ARCHAEOLOGICAL SURVEY OF NORTHERN INDIA (VOL. VI)

MONOGRAPH

ON

BUDDHA SAKYAMUNI'S BIRTH PLACE

IN

THE NEPALESE TARAI

ARCHAEOLOGICAL SURVEY OF NORTHERN INDIA (VOL. VI)

MONOGRAPH ON BUDDHA SAKYAMUNI'S BIRTH PLACE IN THE NEPALESE TARAI

BY

A. FUHRER, PH.D.,
ARCHAEOLOGICAL SURVEYOR,
NORTH-WESTERN PROVINCES AND OUDH.

GYAN

Published by

GYAN

Gyan Publishing House
5, Ansari Road
Daryaganj, New Delhi-110002
Phone: 011-47034999, 9811692060
E-mail: books@gyanbooks.com

Distribution Network
gyanbooks.com
India, USA, Canada, UK, Australia, France

ISBN : 978-81-212-2646-2 (HB)
First Published, 1897

2nd Impression 2021

Printed at: Gyan Press, Delhi.

Monograph
on
Buddha Sakyamuni's Birth Place
Author: A. Fuhrer

ARCHÆOLOGICAL SURVEY OF NORTHERN INDIA VOL. VI.

MONOGRAPH

ON

Buddha Sakyamuni's Birth-Place

IN

THE NEPALESE TARAI.

BY

A. FÜHRER, PH.D.,

ARCHÆOLOGICAL SURVEYOR, NORTH-WESTERN PROVINCES AND OUDH.

ALLAHABAD:

PRINTED AT THE GOVERNMENT PRESS, N.-W. P. AND OUDH.

Calcutta: NEWMAN & Co.; THACKER, SPINK & Co. *Bombay:* THACKER & Co., "LD."

Madras: HIGGINBOTHAM & Co.

London: W. H. ALLEN & Co.; KEGAN PAUL, TRENCH, TRÜBNER & Co.

1897.

PLATE I.

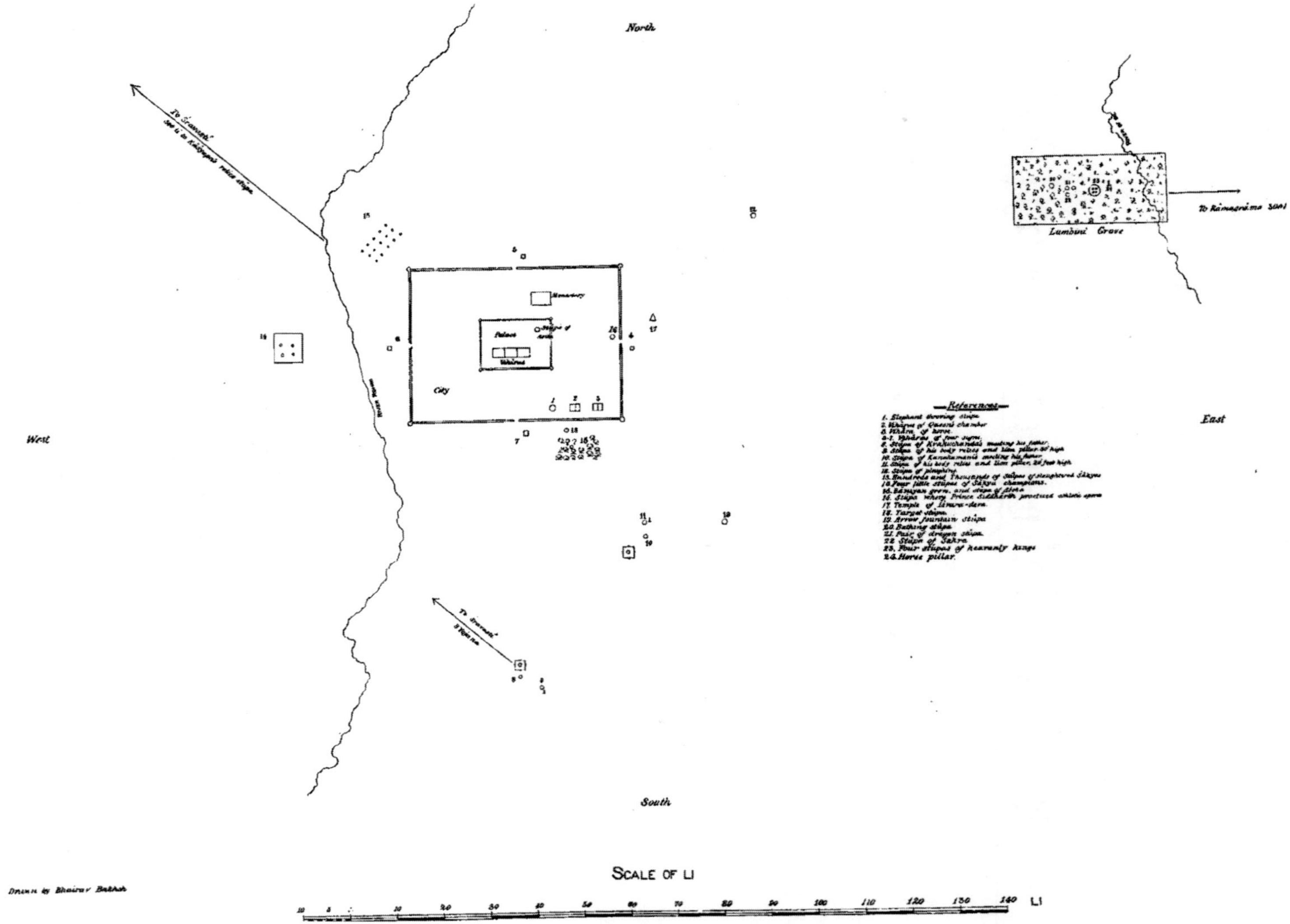
North
South
East
West
Lumbini Grove
City
Palace
Monastery
References
1. Elephant throwing stūpa
2. Vihāra of Queen's chamber
13. Hundreds and Thousands of stūpas of slaughtered Śākyas
14. Four little stūpas of Śākya champions.
16. Stūpa where Prince Siddhārtha practised athletic sports
18. Target stūpa.
19. Arrow fountain stūpa
20. Bathing stūpa
21. Pair of dragon stūpa.
22. Stūpa of Śakra
23. Four stūpas of heavenly kings
24. Horse pillar.
SCALE OF LI
Drawn by Bhairav Bakhsh

List of Volumes constituting the New Imperial Series of the Reports of the Archæological Survey of India.

Prescribed number in New Series.	Name of Book.	Author or Editor.	Date of publication.	*Existing Provincial Number.* Western India.	Southern India.	Northern India.
I	Report of the first season's Operations in the Belgaum and Kaladgi Districts	Burgess	1874 ...	I	...	...
II	Report on the Antiquities of Kathiawar and Kachh ...	Do. ...	1876 ...	II	...	...
III	Report on the Antiquities of the Bidar and Aurangabad Districts.	Do. ...	1878 ...	III	...	...
IV	The Buddhist Caves and their Inscriptions	Do. ...	1883 ...	IV	...	...
V	The Caves of Ellora and the other Brahmanical and Jaina Caves in Western India ...	Do. ...	1884 ...	V	...	...
VI	The Buddhist Stupas of Amaravati and Jaggayyapeta ...	Do. ...	1887 ...	...	I	...
VII	Lists of Antiquarian Remains in the Presidency of Madras (Volume I)	Sewell ...	1882 ...	...	II	...
VIII	Lists of Inscriptions and Sketch of Dynasties of Southern India (Volume II)	Do. ...	1884 ...	...	III	...
IX	South Indian Inscriptions (Volume I)	Hultzsch	1890 ...	...	IV	...
X	South Indian Inscriptions (Volume II)	Do. ...	1891-92	...	V	...
XI	Report on the Sharqi Architecture of Jaunpur	Führer & Smith.	1889 ...	...	...	I
XII	Monumental Antiquities and Inscriptions in the North-Western Provinces and Oudh ...	Führer ...	1891 ...	...	...	II
XIII	Epigraphia Indica (Volume I) ...	Burgess	1891 ...	...	...	...
XIV	Epigraphia Indica (Volume II)...	Do. ...	1894 ...	...	...	...
XV	South Indian Buddhist Antiquities	Rea ...	1894 ...	...	VI	...
XVI	Revised Lists of Antiquarian Remains in the Bombay Presidency	Cousens...	1897 ...	VIII	...	...

Prescribed number in New Series.	Name of Book.	Author or Editor.	Date of publication.	Existing Provincial Number.		
				Western India.	Southern India.	Northern India.
XVII	Lists of Architectural and Archæological Remains in Coorg ...	Rea ...	1894 ...	...	VII	...
XVIII	Report on the Moghal Architecture of Faṭhpur-Sikri, Part I ...	Smith ...	1895 ...	...	...	III
"	Report on the Moghal Architecture of Faṭhpur-Sikri, Part II ...	Do. ...	1896 ...	...	...	III
"	Report on the Moghal Architecture of Faṭhpur-Sikri, Part III	Do. ...	1897 ...	...	...	III
XIX	Lists of Antiquarian Remains in the Central Provinces and Berars	Cousens...	1897 ...	...	...	IV
XX	Monograph on Ancient Jaina Art and Architecture ...	Führer ...	1897 ...	...	...	V
XXI	Chalukyan Architecture, including examples from the Bellary District, Madras Presidency ...	Rea ...	1896 ...	...	VIII	...
XXII	The Bower Manuscript, Part I ...	Hoernle...	1893 ...	...	...	...
"	Ditto, Part II, Fasciculi I and II ...	Do. ...	1894-95	...	...	...
"	Ditto, Parts III—VII...	Do. ...	1897 ...	...	...	...
XXIII	Muhammadan Architecture of Bharoch, Cambay, Dholka, Champanir and Mahmudabad in Gujarat	Burgess...	1897 ...	VI	...	...
XXIV	The Muhammadan Architecture of Ahmadabad	Do. ...	...	VII	...	...
XXV	The Monumental Remains of the Dutch East India Company in the Presidency of Madras ...	Rea ...	1897 ...	...	IX	...
XXVI	Monograph on Buddha Śâkyamuni's Birth-place in the Nepalese Tarâi	Führer ...	1897...	...	...	VI

Mysore Archæological Series.

Number of Volumes.	Name of Book.	Author or Editor.	Date of publication.
I	Coorg Inscriptions	Rice ...	1886.
II	Inscriptions at Sravana Belgola (Epigraphia Carnatica)	Do. ...	1889.
III	Inscriptions in the Mysore District, Part I ...	Do. ...	1894.
IV	Ditto ditto, Part II ...	Do. ...	In the Press.
V	Ditto Hassan District	Do. ...	Ditto.
VI	Ditto Kadur District	Do. ...	Ditto.
VII	Ditto Shemoga District, Part I ...	Do. ...	Ditto.
VIII	Ditto ditto, Part II ...	Do. ...	Ditto.
IX	Ditto Bangalore District	Do. ...	Ditto.
X	Ditto Kolar District	Do. ...	Ditto.
XI	Ditto Chitaldroog District	Do. ...	Ditto.
XII	Ditto Tumkur District	Do. ...	Ditto.

ARCHÆOLOGICAL SURVEY OF INDIA.

NEW IMPERIAL SERIES.

VOLUME XXVI.

NORTHERN INDIA.

VOLUME VI.

THE BUDDHA'S BIRTH-PLACE.

Behold ye now this monk austere,
His matted locks, his penance fierce;
From the fair town called Kapila
His great retirement shall be made.

The mother that shall bring him forth,
Shall Mahâmâyâ be by name;
Śuddhodana his father's name,
His own name shall be Gautama.

[Introduction to the *Jâtaka*, or Book of "Buddha's Birth-stories."]

CONTENTS.

LIST OF PLATES.

PREFACE.

THE aim of this Monograph is to present at an early date to the student of Indian Early History and of Buddhism the results of the important and interesting discoveries made in the Nepâlese Tarâi, north-east of the Basti district of the North-Western Provinces, in the beginning of last camping season.

On the 12th May and the 29th June 1896 I applied through the Government of the North-Western Provinces and Oudh to the Government of India in the Foreign Department, for the favour of its obtaining the sanction of the Khatmandu Darbâr to an exploration being made of the ruins near Niglîvâ as far as Bhagvânpur, fifteen miles east-south-east of Taulihvâ, where I had learned another pillar bearing a supposed Aśoka inscription was still standing. On the 29th August last the Government of India, in its letter No. 1508E.B., informed the Resident at Nepâl: "It has been decided that, if the Nepâl Darbâr grant the necessary permission, Dr. A. Führer, Archæological Surveyor, North-Western Provinces and Oudh, will be deputed to conduct the explorations." In his letter No. $\frac{57P}{17-4055}$, dated the 7th September 1896, to the address of the Secretary to the Government of India in the Foreign Department, Colonel H. Wylie, C.S.I., the Resident at Nepâl, wrote in reply: "His Excellency the Prime Minister has informed me that his brother General Khaḍga Shamsher, Governor of Pâlpa, would be directed to meet Dr. Führer at Niglîvâ, and would be ready to receive suggestions from him regarding the contemplated excavation amongst the ruins of Buddha Koṇâgamana's Nirvâṇa Stûpa."

Convinced of the importance of the proposed explorations of the ruins near Niglîvâ, Herr Hofrat Dr. George Bühler, C.I.E., Professor of Oriental Languages at the University of Vienna, in September 1896, asked some of his friends to contribute about eight hundred rupees towards the expenses likely to be incurred on the above proposal, without attaching any conditions to this liberal gift. As, however, the Nepâl Government had expressed the intention of itself undertaking the excavation operations amongst these ruins, and as my duties in connection with the researches were to be confined to giving advice and making suggestions, no advantage could be taken of the contributions so generously offered from Europe for the laudable object of carrying on the excavations.

That I have accomplished what I did is owing chiefly to the courtesy and magnanimity of the present enlightened Government of Nepâl. All students of Ancient Indian History and all devout Buddhists of India, Ceylon, Burma and the Far East are indebted to His Highness Mahârâja Sir Bir Shamsher Jang Râṇa Bahâdur, G.C.S.I., and to his brother General Khaḍga Shamsher, for the enthusiasm displayed and the great assistance rendered in the successful exploration of these ruins. The Governor of the Tarâi, General Khaḍga Shamsher, who, at my suggestion, had kindly the Rummindei Pillar excavated, did not think any other operations feasible on account of the severe famine from which the Tarâi was then suffering;

but he has generously promised to employ this winter a large number of his Sappers on more extensive excavations, which, if conducted in a systematic and scientific manner, are sure to furnish us with documents and monuments not only of the third century B.C., but of a much earlier period, extending to about the fifth or sixth century before Christ.

In conclusion, I tender my warmest thanks to Bâbu Shohrat Singh, Honorary Magistrate of Chandapâr and Shohratganj in the Basti district, an influential and public-spirited land-proprietor on the Indo-Nepâl frontier, for his great generosity of allowing me the use of two valuable elephants, without which it would have been an almost fruitless task to explore the dense sâl forests in which these interesting ruins are hidden away.

A. FÜHRER.

LUCKNOW MUSEUM,
The 31*st May* 1897.

THE BUDDHA'S BIRTH-PLACE IN THE NEPALESE TARAI.

CHAPTER I.

THE BIRTH OF PRINCE GAUTAMA SIDDHARTHA, THE BUDDHA ŚÂKYAMUNI.

THE history of the Buddha, such as may be extracted from the sacred Pâli books, is so marvellous that all who are standing outside the pale of Buddhism reject more or less its truthfulness. A few of the Western scholars have gone to such lengths as to see in that history the remoulding of an ancient solar myth; others, less radical, are of opinion that it will be possible, by stripping the tale of its miraculous and mythical elements, to find out the historic nucleus. Those are apt to believe that by the aid of their critical manipulations they can produce an image which is extremely like the original. Without denying the worth of critical disquisitions or entering into the merits of the different reconstructions of the traditional history, we must limit ourselves in this chapter to a condensed account of the principal facts in the career of the Sublime Being, whom all Buddhists acknowledge and revere as their Lord *(Bhagavat)* and as the fountain-head of all *Dharmas*; who, according to his own words, throughout myriads of ages had prepared himself, out of charity, before becoming a Buddha, to free sentient beings from the misery of existence. The history of *that* Buddha may be said to be true in an ideal sense.[1]

In reading the canonical Scriptures one is impressed with the strong personal influence exercised by the Buddha over the hearts of his followers. He was regarded not as a mere formulator of dry metaphysical propositions, but as a very wise and compassionate friend of his fellowmen. He was full of tact, and all his ways were ways of peace. To allay discord he would tell a little story or fable with a moral, chosen out of the old Indian folk-lore and adapted to his instructional purposes, and his epithet for one of whom he disapproved was merely "vain man." Anger, in fact, had no place in his character, and it had equally none in his religio-philosophic system. The Buddha may be wrong in his teleology, but his moral code can only be compared with that of Christ, and even Barthelémy Saint-Hilaire cannot but admit "que, sauf le Christ tout seul, il n'est point, parmi les fondateurs de religion, de figure plus pure ni plus touchante que celle du Bouddha, sa vie n'a point de tâche."[2] Look only at the beautiful tale that opens the *Râjovâda Jâtaka*, and

[1] H. Kern, *Manual of Indian Buddhism*, Strassburg, 1896, page 12.

[2] *Le Bouddha et sa Religion*, nouvelle édition, Introduction, page V.

wherein a man's superiority is judged by his way of retaliating. When Confucius was asked: "What do you say concerning the principle that injury should be recompensed with kindness?" the Master said: "With what then will you recompense kindness?"[1] But Christ said unto us: "Love your enemies, bless them that curse you, do good to them that hate you, and pray for them which despitefully use you, and persecute you" (*St. Matthew*, v. 44). And now what does the Buddha teach? Exactly the same as Christ. Of two kings, one "the Kosala-King, by name Mallika, overthrows the strong by strength, the soft by softness, the good he conquers by goodness, the wicked by wickedness; but the other, "the King of Benares, called Brahmadatta, by calmness conquers anger, the wicked he conquers by goodness, he conquers avarice by charity, by truth the false-speaker;" and the latter is by the Buddha[2] deemed the greater. So we, too, say, the more we learn to know the Buddha, the more we love and admire him; and the sooner all mankind shall have been acquainted with his doctrines, the better it will be, for he is certainly one of the heroes of humanity.

The term *Buddha* means "Enlightened One," and signifies that the person to whom it is applied has solved the riddle of existence, and discovered the doctrine for the cessation of misery. It was by his attainment of this supreme "Enlightenment" or Wisdom that the warrior prince Gautama became a Buddha. During the thirty-five years of his life previous to that event, and during all previous existences from the time he set out towards Buddhaship, he was a Bodhisattva—a term which, freely translated, means "Future Buddha," but which is more literally rendered "He whose essence is Wisdom." The Buddha's personal name appears to have been Siddhârtha; but as the word means "Successful in his aim," it looks as though it might be a simple epithet. The Buddha belonged to the Śâkya clan. The word *Śâkya* means "Powerful," and the families that bore the name had a reputation for pride and haughtiness; they were of the warrior caste *(khattiyajâti)*, but cultivated the peaceful arts of agriculture. By his contemporaries the Buddha is usually called the Ascetic Gautama; it is not quite clear why he and others of his clan should bear this family cognomen in addition to the clan-name of Śâkya. It may be they claimed descent from the ancient sage Gautama, to whom are attributed some of the hymns of the *Rigveda;* or it may be, as Burnouf has suggested, "because Gautama was the sacerdotal family name of the military race of the Śâkyas, who, being of the warrior caste, had no ancestor or tutelar saint like the Brâhmans, but might, as the Hindu law permits, have taken the name of the sage to whose family belonged their spiritual guide." The Buddha was born a Hindu, and the religion his parents professed was Śaivism of the ordinary type, as the new born child was brought to the temple, where the goddess Abhayâ bowed down at his feet. During his long ministry of forty-five years he wandered about from place to place in that section of the country which is known as *Madhyadeśa*,[3] very much as did Christ in

---

[1] Legge, *Chinese Classics*, Volume I, page 152. [2] Fausböll, *Ten Jâtakas* (1872), pages 4 and 5.

[3] The Buddhist *Madhyadeśa* lies to the east of Madhyadeśa properly so called; it is, in reality, the *Prâgdeśa*. It is geographically impossible that in any period of Indian History Eastern Hindustân was looked upon as the central region of the Aryan Indians. *See* Note 2, page 3.

Samaria and Judæa. And just as Christ once left his native country and went to Egypt, so the Buddha is said by native authorities to have paid a couple of visits to Ceylon; but the statement is somewhat mythical. The date of Gautama Buddha is considered to be the sixth century before Christ. It would appear that he lived to his eightieth year, and the time of his death is given by scholars as about 477 B.C.

After having exercised the thirty *pâramitâs*, (*i.e.*, the Ten Perfections, each of them divided into three degrees, *see* page 14, Note 1), in anterior births, the Bodhisattva destined to become an omniscient Buddha was born in the Tushita heaven.[1] At the request of the deities, urging him to release mankind, he made, before giving his assent, five examinations: (1) of the time of his appearance, (2) of the continent, (3) of the country, (4) of the race and family, and (5) of the mother who should bear him, and her span of life. He saw that the proper time had arrived; that all Buddhas are born on the continent of India *(Jambudvîpa)* in the Middle country *(Madhyadeśa*[2]*)*; that the Buddhas are born either in the Brâhman or warrior caste; the latter being at the time held in higher estimation, he resolved upon becoming the son of Śuddhodana, the King of the Śâkya clan in Kapilavastu; finally, he saw that the Queen Mahâmâyâ should be his mother and that she should die seven days after his birth. He entered the Nandana Grove of the Tushita capital, Indra's paradise; and here the gods said: "Attain in your next existence your high destiny," and kept reminding him that he had already paved the way to it by his accumulated merit. Now it was while he was thus dwelling, surrounded by these deities, and continually reminded of his accumulated merit, that he died, and was conceived in the womb of Mahâmâyâ. For it was on the last day of the Midsummer Festival (the full-moon day of *Âshâḍha*) in Kapilavastu that Mahâmâyâ had a dream, in which she saw how the Bodhisattva—who in the shape of a white elephant was wandering on Gold Hill in the Himâlaya Mountains—approached her from the North, and seemed to enter her womb. When the Queen next morning told her dream to the King, he summoned sixty-four eminent Brâhmans, interpreters of dreams, who declared that she had conceived a son destined to become either a Universal Monarch or a Buddha, "who will roll back the clouds of sin and folly of this world." Now the instant that the Bodhisattva was conceived in the womb of his mother, all the ten thousand worlds suddenly quaked, quivered and shook. And the thirty-two prognostics appeared as follows: an immeasurable light spread through the thousand worlds; the blind recovered their sight, as if from desire to see this his glory; the deaf received their hearing; the dumb talked; the hunchbacked became straight of body; the lame recovered the power to walk; all those in bonds were freed from their bonds and chains; the fires went out in all the hells; the hunger and thirst of the Manes was stilled;

---

[1] The following authentic narrative is mainly based upon the *Nidânakathâ* or Introduction to the canonical *Jâtaka, together with its Commentary*, 5 Volumes (1877—1891), edited by V. Fausböll; T. W. Rhys Davids, *Buddhist Birth Stories*, London, 1880, pages 1—104; H. C. Warren, *Buddhism in Translations*, Cambridge, Mass., 1896, pages 38—83.

[2] The Middle country is defined in the *Vinayapiṭakam* as follows:—"It lies in the middle, on this side of the town Kajaṅgala on the east, beyond which is Mahâsâlâ, and beyond that the border districts. It lies in the middle, on this side of the river Salalavatî on the south-east, beyond which are the border districts. It lies in the middle, on this side of the town Setakaṇṇika on the south, beyond which are the border districts. It lies in the middle, on this side of the Brâhmanical town Thûṇa on the west, beyond which are the border districts. It lies in the middle, on this side of the hill Usîraddhaja on the north, beyond which are the border districts. It is 300 leagues in length, 250 in breadth, and 900 in circumference."

wild animals lost their timidity: diseases ceased among men; all mortals became mild-spoken; horses neighed and elephants trumpeted in a manner sweet to the ear; all musical instruments gave forth their sounds without being played upon; bracelets and other ornaments jingled; in all quarters of the heavens the weather became fair; a mild, cool breeze began to blow, very refreshing to men; rain fell out of season[1]; water burst forth from the earth and flowed in streams; the birds ceased flying through the air; the rivers checked their flowing; in the mighty ocean the water became smooth; the ground became everywhere covered with lotuses of the five different colours; all flowers bloomed, both those on land and those that grow in the water; a shower of flowers fell all about; celestial music was heard to play in the sky; and the whole ten thousand worlds became one mass of garlands of the utmost possible magnificence, with waving *chauris*, and saturated with the incense-like fragrance of flowers, and resembled a bouquet of flowers sent whirling through the air, or a closely woven wreath, or a superbly decorated altar of flowers.

From the time the Bodhisattva was thus conceived, four celestials with swords in their hands kept guard, to ward off all harm from both the Future Buddha and his mother. When the time of her confinement drew near, Mahâmâyâ grew desirous of going home to her relatives, and said to King Śuddhodana: "Sire, I should like to visit my kinsfolk in their city D e v a d a h a." "So be it," said the king; and from Kapilavastu to the city of Devadaha he had the road made even, and garnished it with plantain-trees set in pots and with banners and streamers; and, seating the queen in a golden palanquin borne by a thousand of his courtiers, he sent her away in great pomp. Now between the two cities, and belonging to the inhabitants of both, was a pleasure-grove of *sâl* trees, called L u m b i n î grove. And at this particular time this grove was one mass of flowers from the ground to the topmost branches, while amongst the branches and flowers hummed swarms of bees of the five different colours, and flocks of various birds flew about warbling sweetly. Throughout the whole of the Lumbinî grove the scene resembled the Chittalatâ grove in Indra's paradise, or the magnificently decorated banqueting pavilion of some potent king. When the queen beheld it, she became desirous of disporting herself therein, and the courtiers therefore took her into it. And going to the foot of the monarch *sâl* tree of the grove, she wished to take hold of one of its branches. And the sâl-tree branch, like the tip of a tender reed, bent itself down within reach of the queen's hand. Then she stretched out her hand, and seized hold of the branch, and immediately her pains came upon her. Thereupon the people hung a curtain about her, and retired. So her delivery took place while she was standing up,[2] and keeping fast hold of the sâl-tree branch. At that very moment came four pure-minded Mahâ-Brahma gods bearing a golden net, and, receiving the Future Buddha

[1] At present the month Âshâḍha, in which the conception took place, falls in the rainy season.

According to the *Lalitavistara* (ed. *Bibl. Ind.*, page 63) the conception takes place at fullmoon day of the month Vaiśâkha, the moon standing in Pushya or Tishya.

The conception is represented in the Bharhut sculpture (Plate XXVIII), inscribed *Bhagavato okamti; see* Cunningham, *The Stûpa of Bharhut.*

[2] The *Jâtaka* adduces the following reasons:—"Other women sometimes fall short of and sometimes run over the term of ten lunar [*i.e.*, the nine calendar] months, and then bring forth either sitting or lying down; but not so the mother of a Bodhisattva. She carries the future Buddha in her womb as it were oil in a vessel, just for ten months, and then brings forth while standing up. This is a characteristic of the mother of a Bodhisattva."

The *Lalitavistara* says that the child was born from the right side of his mother.

on this golden net, they placed him before his mother and said: "Rejoice, oh Queen! A mighty son has been born to you."

Other mortals on issuing from the maternal womb are smeared with disagreeable impure matter; but not so the Future Buddha. He issued from his mother's womb like a preacher descending from his preaching-seat, or a man coming down a stair, stretching out both hands and both feet, unsmeared by any impurity from his mother's womb and flashing pure and spotless like a jewel thrown upon a garment of Benares brocade. Notwithstanding this, for the sake of honouring the Future Buddha and his mother, there came two streams of water from the sky, and refreshed the Bodhisattva and his mother. Then the Brahma celestials, after receiving him on their golden net, delivered him to the four guardian gods of the quarters, who received him from their hands on a rug which was made of the skins of black antelopes and was soft to the touch, being such as is used on State occasions; and the guardian gods delivered him to men who received him on a coil of fine cloth: and the men let him out of their hands on the ground, where he stood and faced the east. There, before him, lay many thousands of worlds like a great open court; and in them, gods and men, making offerings to him of perfumes, garlands and so on, were saying—"Great Being! There is none your equal, much less your superior." When he had in this manner surveyed the four cardinal points, and the four intermediate ones, and the zenith, and the nadir, in short, all the ten directions in order, and had nowhere discovered his equal, he exclaimed, "This is the best direction," and strode forward seven paces, followed by Mahâ-Brahma holding over him the white umbrella, Suyâma bearing the fan, and other divinities having the other symbols of royalty in their hands. Then at the seventh stride he halted, and with a noble voice, he shouted the shout of victory, beginning—"The foremost am I in all the world." Then the inhabitants of both cities took the Bodhisattva, and carried him to Kapilavastu.

On the same day that the Bodhisattva was born in the Lumbinî Grove there also came into existence Yaśodharâ (also called Bimbâ, Gopâ or Yaśovatî) the mother of (the Buddha's son) Râhula, Chanda the courtier, Kâlodâyin the courtier, Kaṇṭhaka the king of horses, and Ânanda (the Buddha's cousin); at the same time sprung into existence the great Bodhi Tree and the four treasure vases. Northern sources name as born at the same time four kings, who play a prominent part in the history of the Buddha, *viz.* Bimbisâra, Prasenajit, Pradyota and Udayana.

The birth of the Bodhisattva caused great rejoicing in the heaven of the thirty-three gods, "because to king Śuddhodana in Kapilavastu had been born a son who shall sit at the foot of the Bodhi Tree and become a Buddha, and cause the Wheel of the Doctrine to roll." The seer Kâladevala (*alias* Asita)—an intimate friend of king Śuddhodana—who happened to witness those rejoicings and on inquiry was informed of the happy event, descended from the world of the gods in haste and entered the palace of the king; and having seated himself on the seat assigned to him he said—"Great king, I hear that a son has been born to you. I would like to see him." Then the king had the prince magnificently dressed and brought in and carried up to do reverence to the venerable ascetic. But the feet of the Future Buddha turned and planted themselves in the matted locks of the ascetic. For in that birth there was no one worthy of the Bodhisattva's reverence; "and if these ignorant people had succeeded in causing the Future Buddha to bow, the head of the ascetic would have split in seven pieces." "It is not meet that I compass my own death," thought the ascetic, and rose from his seat, and with joined hands did reverence to the Bodhisattva. And when the king had seen this wonder, he also did reverence to his son. Noting on the body all the lucky marks and characteristics, the sage prophetically foresaw that the child one day would become a Buddha, but that he himself would die before that time. This afflicted him and he wept. In order to secure to one of his relatives the blessing he was to be deprived of, he went to his sister's son, N â l a k a, and said to the lad: "My child, a son has been born in the family of Śuddhodana the king, who is the coming Buddha; thirty-five years from now he will become a Buddha, and you will have an opportunity of seeing him. Retire from this world this very day." Although belonging to a family possessing eight hundred and seventy millions of treasure, Nâlaka took up the life of a *śramaṇa*, heard afterwards the Master, entered the Order, reached Arhatship and finally *nirvâṇa* (extinction). Five days after the birth of the Bodhisattva, the rite of choosing a name for him was performed, and after bathing his head, he received the name of S i d d h â r t h a or S a r v â r t h a s i d d h a. They prepared the royal palace by anointing it with four kinds of perfumes and by scattering blossoms and flowers, five sorts in all. And making some porridge of whole rice-grains boiled in milk, they invited one hundred and eight Brâhmans, men who had mastered the three Vedas. And having seated these Brâhmans in the royal palace and fed them with delicate food and showed them every attention, they asked them to observe the marks and characteristics of the Bodhisattva's person and to prophesy his future destiny. Among these Brâhmans were eight renowned soothsayers, being the same who had interpreted the dream of the night of the conception. Seven of these raised two fingers each; and gave a double interpretation, saying, "If a man possessing such marks and characteristics continue in the household life, he becomes a Universal Monarch; if he retire from the world, he becomes a Buddha." And then they set forth all the glory of a Universal Monarch. But the youngest of them all, a youth whose clan-name was K a u ṇ ḍ i n y a, raised only one finger and gave but a single interpretation, saying, "There is here naught to make him stay in the household life. He will most undoubtedly become a Buddha and remove the veil of ignorance and folly from the world." For, this Kauṇḍinya was one who had made an earnest wish under former Buddhas, and was now in his last existence. Therefore it was that he outstripped the other seven in knowledge and saw but one future; inasmuch as a person possessed of such marks and characteristics would never stay in the household life, but would undoubtedly become a Buddha. So he raised only one finger, and gave that interpretation. This Brâhman Kauṇḍinya was the very same who afterwards took the vows and became then chief of the "Band of Five Elders" (P a ñ c h a v a g g i y a).

The king, anxious to prevent his son from forsaking the world, asked what would move the Prince to flee from worldly enjoyments. The answer was—"Four ominous signs: a decrepit old man, a diseased man, a dead man, and a monk." "From this time forth," said the king, "let no such persons be allowed to come near my son. It will never do for my son to become a Buddha. What I wish to see is my son exercising sovereign rule and authority over the four great continents and the two thousand attendant isles, and walking through the heavens surrounded by a retinue thirty-six leagues in circumference." And when he had so spoken, he placed guards for a distance of a quarter of a league in each of the four directions. in order that none of the four kinds of men might come within sight of his son. On the same day also eighty thousand clansmen assembled together in the festival-hall, and each dedicated a son, saying "Whether the young prince becomes a Buddha or a king, we will each one give a son: so that if he becomes a Buddha, he shall be followed and surrounded by monks of the warrior caste; and if he becomes a king, by nobles of the warrior caste."

Whereas a womb that has been occupied by a Bodhisattva is like the shrine of a temple, and can never be occupied or used again, therefore it was that Mahâmâyâ, the mother of the Future Buddha, died when he was seven days old, and was reborn in the Tushita heaven.

And the king procured nurses for the Bodhisattva, women of fine figure and free from all blemish. And so the future Buddha grew up under the fostering care of his aunt and step-mother, Mahâ-Prajâpatî Gautamî, surrounded by an immense retinue and in great splendour.

Now on a certain day the king celebrated the Sowing Festival. On that day the people used to decorate the whole city, so that it looked like a palace of the gods; and all the slaves and other servants would put on new garments, and, perfumed and garlanded, they would assemble together at the king's palace where a thousand ploughs were yoked for the royal ploughing. On this occasion there were one hundred and eight ploughs, all save one ornamented with silver, as were also the reins for the oxen and the cross-bars of the ploughs. But the plough that was held by the king was ornamented with red gold as also the horns, the reins and goads for the oxen. And the king issued forth with a large retinue, taking his son along with him. And in the field where the ploughing was to be done was a solitary rose-apple tree *(Eugenia jambu)* of thick foliage and dense shade. Underneath this tree the king had a couch placed for the young prince and spread over his head a canopy that was studded with golden stars; and he surrounded him with a screen and appointed those that should watch by him; and then, decked with all his ornaments and surrounded by his courtiers, he proceeded to the place where they were to plough. On arriving there, the king took the golden plough, and the courtiers took the (107) silver ploughs and the farmers the other ploughs: and then all ploughed forward and backward. The king went from the hither side to the farther side and from the farther side back again: and the pomp and the magnificence of the festival was at its climax. Now the nurses who were sitting about the Bodhisattva came out from behind the screen to behold the royal magnificence. And the prince, looking hither and thither and seeing no one, arose in haste and sat down cross-legged, and, mastering his inspirations and expirations, entered on the first trance.[1] The nurses delayed a little, being detained by the abundance of good things to eat. And the shadows of the other trees passed over to the east, but the shadow of the jambu-tree remained steadily circular. Suddenly the nurses remembered that they had left their young master alone, and, raising the screen, they entered and saw the Bodhisattva sitting cross-legged on the couch, and also noticed the miracle of the shadow. Then they went and announced the miracle to the king, who came in all haste and prostrated himself before his son, saying—"This, dear child, is my second obeisance."

On reaching the age of sixteen years, Prince Siddhârtha was married to Yaśodharâ, the daughter of Suprabuddha, his own cousin. And the king built three palaces for them, suited to the three seasons—one of nine, another of seven, and another of five stories. And he provided him with forty thousand dancing girls. And the Future Buddha, with his gaily dressed dancers, was like a god surrounded by hosts of nymphs, and attended by musical instruments that sounded of themselves; he lived, as the seasons changed, in each of these three palaces.

Now while he was thus enjoying great splendour, one day there arose the following discussion among his relatives:—"Siddhârtha is wholly given up to pleasure and is not training himself in any manly art. What could he do if war were to occur?" The king sent for the Prince and said: "My child, your relatives are saying that you are not training yourself, but are wholly given up to pleasure. Now what do you think we had best do?" "Sire, I do not need to train myself. Let the crier go about the city, beating the drum, to announce that I will show my proficiency to my relatives on the seventh day from now." The king did so. And the Bodhisattva assembled together bowmen that could shoot like lightning and at a hair's breadth: and in the midst of the populace, and before his kinsfolk, he exhibited a twelvefold skill such as none of the other bowmen could equal. So the assembly of his kinsfolk doubted him no longer.

Time passed on, and the Bodhisattva lived in luxury and all kinds of enjoyments. On a certain day the Prince ascended his sumptuous and elegant chariot, drawn by four State horses of the Sindh breed, as white as the petals of the white lotus, and drove with his charioteer Chanda to the park. The gods, knowing that the time was approaching when he would attain supreme enlightenment, resolved to show him the four ominous sights. One among the gods assumed the form of an old decrepit man, broken-toothed, gray-haired, crooked and bent of body, leaning on a staff, and trembling. The Prince asked Chanda: "Pray, friend, who is this man?" And when he had heard the answer, he said: "Shame on birth, since to every one that is born old age must come." With emotions in his mind, the Prince quickly returned home, and the king on being informed of the reason of that speedy return, felt his anxiety increase, and doubled the guards surrounding the palace. On another day the Prince saw, under the same circumstances, a sick man produced by the power of the gods. He put the same question, and, on hearing the answer, turned back in agitation. The king multiplied the means of enjoyments for his son, and again

[1] The *Visuddhimagga* (Chapter IV) explains:—"He who isolates himself from sensual pleasure and demeritorious traits, and still exercises reasoning and reflection, enters upon the first trance, which is produced by isolation and characterised by joy and happiness."

doubled the guards. Some time after the Bodhisattva, when driving to the gardens, met with a corpse fashioned by the gods. The answer given by his charioteer moved him more than ever; quickly he returned to the palace, and the king redoubled his precautions. On a fourth occasion, the Bodhisattva on his drive to the park saw by the instrumentality of the gods a monk, carefully and decently clad. He asked his charioteer "Pray, who is this man?" Although there was no Buddha in the world, and the charioteer had no knowledge of either monks or their good qualities, yet by the power of the gods he was inspired to say, "Sire, this is one who has retired from the world;" and he thereupon proceeded to sound the praises of retirement from the world. The thought of retiring from the world was a pleasing one to the Future Buddha, and this day he went on until he came to the park. When he had disported himself there throughout the day, and had bathed in the royal pleasure-tank, he went at sun-set and sat down on the royal resting-stone with the intention of adorning himself. At that instant the throne on which Śakra was sitting grew hot, a certain foreboding of danger to his dominion. Conceiving that the Bodhisattva at midnight of that very day would leave the palace and carry out the Great Renunciation, he ordered Viśvakarman to go to the gardens and adorn Siddhârtha with heavenly attire. By his superhuman power, Viśvakarman came into the presence of the Prince, and disposed in a divine manner the fold of the latter's turban-cloth like a circlet of precious stones. Thus adorned with great richness, the Bodhisattva mounted his superbly-decorated chariot. At this juncture he received the message that Yaśodharâ had been delivered of a son, on hearing which he said, "An impediment *(râhula)* has been born; a fetter has been born." Hence the name of Râhula was given to the child by the order of Śuddhodana.

But the future Buddha in his splendid chariot entered the city with a pomp and magnificence of glory that enraptured all minds At the same moment Kisâ Gautamî, a virgin of the warrior caste, ascended to the roof of her palace, and beheld the beauty and majesty of the Future Buddha as he circumambulated the city; and in her pleasure and satisfaction at the sight she burst forth into this song of joy:—

Quite happy now that mother is,
Quite happy now that father is,
Quite happy now that woman is,
Who owns this lord so glorious.

On hearing this the Future Buddha thought, "In beholding a handsome figure the heart of a mother attains Nirvâṇa, the heart of a father attains Nirvâṇa, the heart of a wife attains Nirvâṇa. This is what she says. But wherein does Nirvâṇa consist?" And to him, whose mind was already averse to passion, the answer came, "When the fire of lust is extinct, that is Nirvâṇa; when the fires of hatred and infatuation are extinct, that is Nirvâṇa: when pride, false belief, and all other passions and torments are extinct, that is Nirvâṇa. She has taught me a good lesson. Certainly, Nirvâṇa is what I am looking for. It behoves me this very day to quit the household life and to retire from the world in quest of Nirvâṇa.[1] I will send

[1] The term rendered by "happy" in Kisâ Gautamî's stanza is *nibbuta*, and Nirvâṇa is synonymous with *nibbuti (nirvṛiti)*. The Future Buddha therefore puns when he pretends that the lady was using *nibbuta* for *nibbuti*, and was urging him to Nirvâṇa.

this lady a teacher's fee." And loosening from his neck a pearl necklace worth a hundred thousand pieces of money, he sent it to Kisâ Gautamî. And great was her satisfaction at this, for she thought "Prince Siddhârtha has fallen in love with me and sent me a present."

The Bodhisattva entered his palace in great splendour and lay on his couch of state. And richly dressed women, skilled in all manner of dance and song, and beautiful as celestial nymphs, gathered around him with all kinds of musical instruments, and with dance, song, and music they endeavoured to please him. But the Prince's aversion to passion did not allow him to take pleasure in the spectacle, and he fell into a brief slumber. And the women exclaiming "he for whose sake we should perform has fallen asleep; of what use is it to weary ourselves any longer?" threw down their various instruments on the ground and lay down. And the lamps fed with sweet-smelling oil continued to burn. And the Future Buddha awoke, and seating himself cross-legged on the couch, perceived these women lying asleep, with their musical instruments scattered about them on the floor, some with their bodies wet with trickling phlegm and spittle: some grinding their teeth and muttering and talking in their sleep; some with their mouths open; and some with their dress fallen apart so as plainly to disclose their loathsome nakedness. This great alteration in their appearance still further increased his aversion for sensual pleasures. To him that magnificent apartment, as splendid as the palace of Śakra, began to seem like a cemetery filled with dead bodies impaled and left to rot; and the three modes of existence appeared like houses all ablaze. And breathing forth the solemn utterance "how oppressive and stifling is it all!" his mind turned ardently to retiring from the world. "It behoves me to go forth on the Great Renunciation *(abhiṇishkramaṇa)* this very day," said he, and arose from his couch, called his charioteer and gave orders to saddle his horse. While Chanda was saddling the steed Kaṇṭhaka, the Bodhisattva went to the room of Râhula's mother. He opened the door and saw Yaśodharâ sleeping with one of her hands upon the head of the child. Fearing that her awakening would be an obstacle to his going away, he silently left the palace. As soon as he came out, he went to his gigantic white courser, bestrode it, and ordered Chanda to take hold of its tail, and so arrived at midnight at the great gate of the city. The king, in order that the Prince should not at any time go out of the city without his knowledge, had caused each of the two leaves of the gate to be made so heavy as to need a thousand men to move it. But the Bodhisattva had a vigour and strength that was equal, when reckoned in elephant-power, to the strength of ten thousand elephants, and, reckoned in man-power, to the strength of a hundred thousand million men. But the city gate was opened by the power of the guardian divinity that inhabited it, and so the Bodhisattva escaped.

At that moment *Mâra*[1] "the Evil One," appeared in the air, with the intention to prevent the Bodhisattva to become a Buddha, by promising him in a week the dignity of a Universal Monarch. But the Prince, not aiming at worldly sovereignty, remained deaf to the Tempter who, baffled in his design, maliciously followed him, like an ever-present shadow, ever on the watch for an opportunity.

[1] The Buddhists recognise no real devil. Mâra, the ruler of the sixth and highest heaven of sensual pleasure, approaches the nearest to our Satan. He stands for the pleasures of sense, and hence is the Buddha's natural enemy.

Then the Future Buddha, casting away with indifference a universal sovereignty already in his grasp, departed from the city in great splendour on the full-moon day of *Âshâḍha*, when the moon was in Libra. At a short distance from the city he turned his face and gazed upon it, and indicated in that place the spot for the "shrine of Kaṇṭhaka's return." Then he turned Kaṇṭhaka in the direction in which he meant to go and proceeded on his way in great pomp and exceeding glory, a host of deities attending him with lighted torches and doing him homage with heavenly perfumes, garlands, sandal-wood powder and incense. And the sky was as full of coral flowers as it is of pouring water at the height of the rainy season. Celestial choruses were heard, and on every side bands of music played: it was as when the storm-clouds thunder on the sea, or when the ocean roars against the Yugandhara rocks. Advancing in this glory, the Bodhisattva in one night passed through three kingdoms, and at the end of thirty *yojanas* he came to the river Anomâ ("Illustrious"). He sprung with his steed over the river, dismounted, and standing on the sandy beach that stretched away like a sheet of silver, said to Chanda: Take these ornaments and Kaṇṭhaka, and go home. I am about to retire from the world." Thereupon the Bodhisattva thought, "These long locks of mine are not suited to a monk; but there is no one fit to cut the hair of a Future Buddha. Therefore I will cut them off myself with my sword." And grasping a scimitar with his right hand, he seized his top-knot with his left hand and cut it off together with the diadem. His hair thus became two finger-breadths in length, and, curling to the right, lay close to his head. As long as he lived it remained of that length, and the beard was proportionate; and never again did he have to cut either hair or beard. Then seizing hold of his hair and diadem, he threw them into the air, saying: "If I am to become a Buddha, let them stay in the sky; but if not, let them fall to the ground." The tuft of hair and jewelled turban went up and remained suspended in the sky, where Śakra received it in an appropriate jewelled casket, and established it in the heaven of the thirty-three gods as the "Shrine of the Diadem." Again the Future Buddha thought: "These garments of mine, made of Benares cloth, are not suited to a monk." At that moment the Mahâ-Brahma god, Ghaṭîkâra, who had been a friend of his in the time of Buddha Kâśyapa, provided him with the eight requisites of a monk, *viz.*, the three robes, the alms-bowl, the razor, needle, the belt and water-strainer. When the Bodhisattva had put on this most excellent vesture, the symbol of saintship and of retirement from the world, he bade Chanda to go back to Kapilavastu with the salutations to his parents. And the charioteer did obeisance to the Bodhisattva, and, keeping his right side towards him, he departed; but the horse Kaṇṭhaka, being unable to bear his grief, died of a broken heart, and was reborn in the heaven of the thirty-three as the god Kaṇṭhaka.

The Bodhisattva, having thus entered upon the life of a recluse, spent a week in the mango grove of Anupiya in the joy of having retired from the world. Thence he travelled in one day on foot to Râjagṛiha, the capital of Magadha, a distance of thirty *yojanas*, and, entering the city, he begged for food from house to house without passing any by. By the beauty of the Future Buddha the whole city was thrown into a state of commotion; and the king, Seniya Bimbisâra, observing the Great Man *(mahâpurusha)* from the roof of his palace, ordered his servants to go and ascertain the nature of the stranger. The men found the Bodhisattva, who, after having collected sufficient food, had left the city by the same gate he had entered, sitting down with his face to the east in the shade of the Pâṇḍava Rock, and eating, not without an effort, his coarse meal. Then the king's men returned and announced what they had seen. And the king, on hearing the report of the messengers, issued hastily from the city, and approaching the Bodhisattva, and being pleased with his deportment, he tendered him all his kingly glory. "Great king," replied the Future Buddha, "I do not seek for the gratification of my senses or my passions, but have retired from the world for the sake of the supreme and absolute enlightenment." "Verily," said the king, when his repeated offers had all been refused, "you are sure to become a Buddha; but when that happens, your first journey must be to my kingdom." Then the Bodhisattva, having made the required promise, proceeded on his way; and coming to Âlâra Kâlâma and Uddaka, disciple of Râma, two renowned teachers of philosophy, he acquired from them the eight stages of ecstatic meditation *(samâpatti)*. But becoming convinced that they did not lead to enlightenment, he ceased to practice them. And being desirous of making the Great Struggle *(mahâpadhâna)*, so as to show the world of gods and men his fortitude and heroism, he went to Uruvilvâ. And saying, "truly, delightful is this spot, enchanting this grove of trees, and this silvery river flows by, easy of approach and delightful, and there is a village near by in which to beg. Truly there is here everything necessary for a youth of good family who is desirous of struggling," he there took up his abode, and began the Great Struggle. Now it came to pass that those five persons, Kauṇḍinya and the others, who, since their retirement from the world, were wandering about for alms through villages, market-towns and royal cities, here met with the Bodhisattva, and resolved to stay with him, persuaded as they were that ere long he would become a Buddha. After six years of exertion, the Bodhisattva resolved to practice the most profound meditation *(dhyâna)* and to perform the most rigid austerities, such as living on one sesamum seed or on one grain of rice a day. By carrying his fasting to excess, his body became emaciated to the last degree and lost its golden colour and became black. One day, when he was deep in a trance of suppressed breathing, he was attacked by violent pains and fell senseless to the ground. Some gods said "the monk Gautama is dead;" others, however, remarked "this is a practice of the Arhats." And indeed, not long afterwards the Bodhisattva recovered his consciousness and stood up. As he perceived that mortification was not the way to enlightenment, he went begging through villages and market-towns for ordinary material food, and lived upon it. This caused "the band of five priests" to lose faith in him; hence they took their bowls and robes and left the Great Man, and going eighteen *yojanas* off they entered Rishipatana in the Deer-park near Benares.

At that time there lived in Uruvilvâ a girl named Sujâtâ, the chieftain's daughter. On the full-moon day of Vaiśâkha, full six years after the Bodhisattva commenced his austerities, she rose up early in the morning to make an offering to a certain banyan-tree, and gave orders to milk the eight cows. Seeing many miracles, she joyfully sent her slave-girl Pûrṇâ to get everything ready under the holy tree. Now that night the Future Buddha had five great dreams, and on considering their meaning, he came to the conclusion that undoubtedly this very day he would become a Buddha. And when night was over, and he had cared for his person, he came early in the morning to that tree, to await the hour to go begging. And when he sat down he illumed the whole tree with his radiance. Then Pûrnâ came and saw the Bodhisattva sitting at the foot of the tree, contemplating the eastern quarter of the world. And when she beheld the radiance from his body lighting up the whole tree with golden colour, she became greatly excited, and ran away in great haste and told Sujâtâ of the matter. When Sujâtâ heard this news, she was overjoyed, and after pouring milk-rice in a golden dish worth a hundred thousand pieces of money, she went to the tree and presented it to the Future Buddha. The earthenware bowl, which he had kept so long and which had been given him by Ghaṭîkâra, at that instant disappeared. The Bodhisattva rose from his seat and walked round the tree with his right side towards it; and taking the dish, he proceeded to the banks of the river Nairañjarâ and descended into its water, just as many thousands of Bodhisattvas before him had descended on the day of their complete enlightenment. The spot where he bathed is now a place of pilgrimage named Suppatiṭṭhita ("well-established"), and here he deposited the dish on the bank before descending into the water. After bathing he dressed himself in that garb of saintship which had been the dress of many hundreds of thousands of Future Buddhas before him; and sitting down with his face to the east, he made the whole of the thick, sweet milk-rice into forty-nine pellets of the size of the fruit of the single-seeded palmyra-tree, and ate it. And he took no further nourishment until the end of the seven weeks or forty-nine days, which he spent on the throne of wisdom, after he had become a Buddha. When he had consumed the milk-rice, he took the golden dish, and saying "If I am to succeed in becoming a Buddha to-day, let this dish go up-stream; but if not, let it go down-stream," he threw it into the water. And, lo, it went up to a great distance, when it sank down to the palace of the Nâga-king Kâla and hit against the dishes that had been used by the last three Buddhas, and took its place at the end of the row. Then the Future Buddha took his noon-day rest on the banks of the river in a grove of *sâl* trees in full bloom. And at nightfall, at the time the flowers droop on their stalks, he rose up like a lion when he bestirs himself, and went towards the Bodhi-tree, along a road which the gods had decked. The snakes, the fairies, the birds and other classes of beings did him homage with celestial perfumes, flowers and other offerings, and celestial choruses poured forth heavenly music: so that the ten thousand worlds were filled with these perfumes, garlands and shouts of acclaim. Just then there came from the opposite direction a grass-cutter, named Sotthiya, and when he saw the Great Man, that he was a holy man, he gave him eight handfuls of grass. He accepted the offering, took a survey of the quarters, and walking round the tree with his right side towards it, he came to the eastern side and faced the west. It is on the eastern side of their Bodhi-trees that all the Buddhas have sat cross-legged, and that side neither trembles nor quakes. Then the Great Man, saying to himself "this is the immovable spot on which all the Buddhas have planted themselves!

This is the place for destroying passion's net," took hold of his handful of grass by one end and shook it out there. And the blades of grass formed themselves into a seat fourteen cubits long, of such symmetry of shape as not even the most skilful painter or carver could design. Then the Bodhisattva turned his back to the trunk of the Bodhi-tree and faced the east. And making the mighty resolution "let my skin and sinews and bones become dry, and let all the flesh and blood in my body dry up! But never from this seat will I stir, until I have attained the supreme and absolute wisdom!" he sat down cross-legged in an unconquerable position, from which not even the descent of a hundred thunderbolts at once could have dislodged him. It was at this point that Mâra exclaiming, "Prince Siddhârtha is desirous of passing beyond my control, but I will never allow it!" summoned his army to do battle. Himself mounted on the elephant Girimekhala ("girded with mountains") led the attack, which was so dreadful that the gods attending the Bodhisattva were seized with terror and fled. The Great Man alone remained undaunted, putting his trust into the Ten Perfections *(pâramitâs)*.[1] Thereupon Mâra caused violent winds to blow, followed by a great rain-storm, showers of rocks, weapons, live coals, hot ashes, sand, mud and darkness. All in vain. Seeing all his attempts baffled, the Fiend approached the Great Man and summoned him to vacate his seat. "Mâra," was the reply, "you have not fulfilled the Ten Perfections in any of their three grades, nor have you made the five great donations,[2] nor have you striven for knowledge, nor for the welfare of the world, nor for enlightenment. This seat does not belong to you, but to me." Enraged at these words, Mâra hurled his discus weapon at him; but the Bodhisattva reflected on the Ten Perfections, and the discus changed into a canopy of flowers, and remained suspended over his head. Then the followers of Mâra began hurling immense mountain-crags; but they were turned into wreaths of flowers, and then fell to the ground. And the Great Man, after his assertion that the seat which Future Buddhas had always used on the day of their complete enlightenment belonged to him, continued and said: "Mâra, who is witness to your having given donations?" Mâra pointed to his army, who with a roar like the roar of an earthquake testified to their master's liberality. In his turn the Fiend asked: "Siddhârtha, who is witness to your having given donations?" Then the Bodhisattva called up the Earth to be his witness, and she replied with such a roaring voice that the hosts of Mâra were discomfited, and the elephant Girimekhala fell down on his knees to do homage to the Great Man. And the followers of Mâra fled in all directions, whereas the gods exultingly shouted "Mâra is defeated! Prince Siddhârtha has conquered! Let us go to celebrate the victory!" And the Nâgas and other celestial beings approached with perfumes, garlands and ointments in their hands to the throne of wisdom, chanting songs of victory.

It was before the sun had set that the Bodhisattva thus vanquished the army of Mâra. And then, while the Bodhi-tree in homage rained red coral-like sprigs upon his priestly robes, he acquired in the first watch of the night the knowledge

[1] The Ten Perfections or Conditions are as follows:—" Alms-giving, keeping the precepts, renunciation, wisdom, courage, patience, truth, resolution, good-will and indifference."

[2] The five great donations are: "The gift of treasure, of child, of wife, of royal rule, and of life and limbs (see *Abhidhânappadîpikâ*, 421)."

of his previous existences *(pûrvanivâsa)*, in the middle watch of the night the divine eye *(divyachakshus)*, and in the last watch of the night his intellect fathomed the knowledge of the series of causes and effect, or dependent origination *(pratîtyasamutpâda)*. While he was musing on the twelve terms *(nidâna)* of Dependent Origination[1] forwards and back, round and back again, the ten thousand worlds quaked twelve times, so far as to their ocean boundaries. And when the Buddha, at the dawning of the day, had thus made the ten thousand worlds thunder with his attainment of omniscience, all these worlds became most gloriously adorned. And when thus he had attained to omniscience, and was the centre of such unparalleled glory and homage, and as many prodigies were happening about him as at his birth, he breathed forth that solemn utterance which had never been omitted by any of the Buddhas:—

Through birth and rebirth's endless round,
Seeking in vain, I hastened on,
To find who framed this edifice.
What misery!—birth incessantly.

O builder! I've discovered thee!
This fabric thou shalt ne'er rebuild!
Thy rafters all are broken now,
And pointed roof demolished lies!
This mind has demolition reached,
And seen the last of all desires.

[1] The Buddha's thoughts were as follows: "On ignorance depends *Karma;* on *Karma* depends consciousness; on consciousness depend name and form; on name and form depend the six organs of sense; on the six organs of sense depends contact; on contact depends sensation; on sensation depends desire; on desire depends attachment; on attachment depends existence; on existence depends birth; on birth depend old age and death, sorrow, lamentation, misery, grief and despair. Thus does this entire aggregation of misery arise."

"But on the complete fading out and cessation of ignorance ceases *Karma;* on the cessation of *Karma* ceases consciousness; on the cessation of consciousness cease name and form; on the cessation of name and form cease the six organs of sense; on the cessation of the six organs of sense ceases contact; on the cessation of contact ceases sensation; on the cessation of sensation ceases desire; on the cessation of desire ceases attachment; on the cessation of attachment ceases existence; on the cessation of existence ceases birth; on the cessation of birth cease old age and death, sorrow, lamentation, misery, grief and despair. Thus does this entire aggregation of misery cease *(see Mahâvagga*, opening sections; *Samyuttanikâya*, Chapter XXII; *Visuddhimagga*, Chapter XVII).

CHAPTER II.

KSHEMAVATÎ, OR NÂBHIKA, THE BIRTH-PLACE OF BUDDHA KRAKUCCHANDA.

It is a common opinion among the European savants that the Buddhas or Tathâgatas[1] preceding Śâkyamuni are mythical, the latter alone being historical. That theory, whether true or false, is entirely opposed to the fixed dogma of historical Buddhism. In the oldest system of it we have cognizance of, the Buddha of the present period had been preceded by twenty-four[2] others. Their names are:— Dîpaṃkara, Koṇḍañña (Kauṇḍinya), Maṅgala, Sumanas, Raivata, Śobhita, Anomadassi (Anavamadarśin), Paduma (Padma), Nârada, Padumuttara (Padmottara), Sumedha, Sujâta, Piyadassin (Priyadarśin) Atthadassin (Arthadarśin), Dhammadassin (Dharmadarśin), Siddhattha (Siddhârtha), Tissa, (Tishya), Phussa (Pushya), Vipassin (Vipaśyin), Sikkhin (Śikhin), Vessabhû (Viśvabhû), Kakusandha, or Kakutsanda (Krakucchanda), Koṇâgamana (Kanakamuni), and Kassapa (Kâśyapa). According to the most authentic record, the *Buddhavaṁśa*, "all these aforetime Buddhas were tranquil and free from every passion. Like the many-rayed sun, they chased away the dense darkness and, having flamed like fire-balls, became extinct with all their train." Each of them has his peculiar *bodhi*-tree, *e.g.*, Dîpaṁkara the *assattha*, or pippal-tree *(Ficus religiosa)*, just as Gautama Buddha; Viśvabhû the *sâl*-tree *(Shorea robusta)*; Kakusandha the *śirîsha (Acacia Sirisa)*, and Koṇâgamana the *udumbara (Ficus glomerata)*. In fact the bas-reliefs of the Bharhut Stûpa,[3] dating back as far as about 250 B. C., show us the bodhi-trees of six out of the last seven Buddhas, *viz.*, those of Vipassi, Vessabhû, Kakuṣandha, Koṇâgamana, Kassapa, and Śâkyamuni with the name of the respective Buddha engraved under each tree. Many of these Tathâgatas are also mentioned in the writings of the Northern schools of Buddhists, but not systematically, and lumped together with others of later invention. The last seven Buddhas are common to the North and the South, and are designated in Northern texts as the *Mânushi-Buddhas*. Sometimes we find that the four last Buddhas, Śâkyamuni included, received special worship. Just as there were twenty-five Tathâgatas in the past, so there will be ten Buddhas in the future. The Buddha of the next following period is Maitreya, or Metteyya, surnamed Ajita, at present still a Bodhisattva living in the Tushita heaven. "All beings who give gifts, keep the precepts, keep fast-days, fulfil their religious duties, found shrines, plant sacred fig-trees, parks and groves, make bridges, clear the highways, take their stand in the precepts of Buddha and dig wells shall see him:" thus says the *Anâgatavaṁśa* or the Buddhist "Apocalypse."

---

[1] The meaning of this term, like that of its Jaina equivalent Tatthâgaya, possibly is "he who has arrived there *(tatra* or *tattha)*, *i.e.*, to emancipation, or *nirvâṇa*." *See* Kern, *l. c.* pages 62—65.

[2] Properly there are three more Buddhas or Tathâgatas, *viz.*, Taṇhaṃkara, Medhaṃkara, and Savaṇaṃkara; but as none of them prophesied concerning the future Buddhaship of Gautama Buddha, they are not taken into account.

[3] Cunningham, *The Stûpa of Bharhut*, Plates XXIX and XXX.

All Tathâgatas are alike, save in a few points of no importance; they differ, for example, in size and in duration of life; some are born as Kshattriyas, others as Brâhmans, *e.g.* Kakusandha, Koṇâgamana, and Kassapa. The Buddhas are never born into a family of the peasant caste, or of the servile caste. Śâkyamuni, the Buddha of the present period, though by birth a Kshattriya, is by genius and conduct a Brâhman. The Law proclaimed by all Tathâgatas is likewise one and the same, and when it is stated that Gautama Buddha evolved the Law from within himself without the aid of a Master, the meaning is that by his intuition he rediscovered the old truths which had been forgotten in the night of dark ages. The Buddhas are the highest spiritual beings; so the supreme Buddha has said himself repeatedly. Among the external characteristics of a Buddha the most remarkable are the thirty-two physical perfections *(mahâpurusha-lakshaṇas)*, which he shares with *Chakravartins*, *Arhats* and other eminent persons, and eighty secondary characteristics *(anuvyañjana)*, most of which are only insignificant modifications of the primary ones. Besides these marks, 216 *mâṅgalya-lakshaṇas*, or "auspicious marks," 108 on each foot, are attributed to the Buddha.[1] It is a remarkable custom of all Buddhas that with their divine eye they survey the world six times every day. As something peculiar to Gautama Buddha, it is recorded that he measured twelve cubits, or as others have it, eighteen cubits in height. This tradition is somewhat countenanced by the dimensions of his sacred footprint, *śrîpâda*, on the Sumana or Adam Peak in Ceylon, described as a superficial hollow more than five feet long and two and a-half feet wide.

The mental characteristics of a Buddha are divided into three categories, each of them comprising a certain sum of qualities, *viz.* (1) the ten forces or powers *(balas)*, (2) the eighteen peculiar properties *(âveṇika-dharmas)*, and (3) the four points of self-confidence or assurance *(vaiśâradyaś)*.

The ten *balas* are: (1) the knowledge of what is fit or unfit; (2) of the necessary consequences of *karma;* (3) of the right road leading to any end; (4) of the elements; (5) of the different inclinations of beings; (6) of the relative powers of the organs; (7) of all degrees of meditations and ecstasy, as well as of their power to purify and fortify the mind; (8) of remembering former births; (9) of descending into the mother's womb and of the birth; (10) of removing moral corruption. On account of these powers a Buddha bears also the epithet of D a ś a b a l a.

The eighteen *âveṇika-dharmas*, otherwise termed *Buddha-dharmas*, or qualities of a Buddha, are the following:—(1) the seeing of all things past; (2) of all things future; (3) of all things present; (4) propriety of actions of the body; (5) of speech; (6) of thought; (7) firmness of intention; (8) of memory; (9) of *samâdhi, i.e.* a state of most intense concentration and absorption; (10) of energy; (11) of emancipation; (12) of wisdom; (13) freedom from fickleness or wantonness; (14) from noisiness; (15) from confusedness; (16) from hastiness; (17) from heedlessness; and (18) from inconsiderateness.

The four *vaiśâradyas* are:—(1) the assurance of the Tathâgata that he has obtained omniscience; (2) that he has free'd himself from sin; (3) that he knows the impediments to Nirvâṇa; and (4) that he has shown the right way to salvation.

[1] For a full description and enumeration of these characteristics, *see* Senart, *Légende de Buddha*, page 149; Burnouf, *Lotus de la bonne loi*, page 622.

Having surveyed the external and internal characteristics of a Buddha, the question arises: "What kind of a being is a Buddha?" The answer is given by the Lord himself. Once upon a time the Brâhman D r o ṇ a, seeing the Lord sitting at the foot of a tree, asked him: "Are you a Deva?" And the Lord answered: "I am not." "Are you a Gandharva?" "I am not." "Are you a Yaksha?" "I am not." "Are you a man?" "I am not a man." On the Brâhman asking what then he might be, the answer was, "know, oh Brâhman, that I am a Buddha." Here the Buddha denies flatly and categorically that he is a man. Consequently, in all periods of the Buddhist creed the Buddha is only anthropomorphic, not a man;[1] what he may have been in pre-historic Buddhism, must be left to individual taste and fancy: it is no matter of science.

It is quite in keeping with Indian habits that the qualities and functions of such a Sublime Being as the Buddha are indicated by a host of epithets and titles, which more or less assume the character of proper nouns. The most common appellations, forming ample material for a complete Buddhology, are:—"All Pitiful, All-Seeing One, Author of all Truth, Best of Men, Blessed Buddha, Blessed One, Chief of Men, Conqueror, Glorious One, Great Man, Great Elect, Great Hero, Great Sage, Great Teacher, Guiltless One, Happy One, Holy One, Leader of the World, Light of the World, Lord, Lord of all the World, Mighty Monk, Mighty Sage, Possessor of the Ten Forces, Fearless One, Radient One, Recipient of Offerings, Reverend Sir *(bhante)*, Saint, Seeing One, Supreme Buddha, Teacher of Gods and Men, Unrivalled, Victor, Victor in the Battle, Who came the good journey which led to Buddhahood, Who has fully accomplished the eight kinds of supernatural knowledge and the fifteen holy practices, Who has arrived at the knowledge of all truth, Who has made subject to him all mortal beings whether in heaven or on earth, Who knows the Universe, Who knew all worlds, and Wise One."

According to the *Buddhavaṁśa*, the Buddha Kakusandha or Krakucchanda (*i.e.* "he who readily solves all doubts") was born at K s h e m â or K s h e m a v a t î in the house of the Brâhman A g n i d a t t a. The Chinese Buddhist monk Fa Hien,[2] who visited India between A.D. 400 and 414, says in his *Travels*—"Going on south-east from the City of Śrâvastî for twelve *yojonas* (about 96 miles) the travellers came to a town named N a - p e i - k e â [*i.e.* N â b h i k a],[3] the birthplace of

[1] The *Jâtaka*, however, has the following gloss: "It is only a human being that can successfully wish to be a Buddha; a serpent, or a bird, or a deity cannot successfully make the wish. Of human beings it is only one of the male sex that can make the wish; it would not be successful on the part of a woman, or of a eunuch, or of a neuter, or of a hermaphrodite. Of men it is he. and only he, who is in a fit condition by the attainment of saintship in that same existence, that can successfully make the wish. Of those in a fit condition it is only he who makes the wish in the presence of a living Buddha that succeeds in his wish; after the death of a Buddha a wish made at a relic-shrine, or at the foot of a Bodhi-tree, will not be successful. Of those who make the wish in the presence of a Buddha it is he, and only he, who has retired from the world that can successfully make the wish, and not one who is a layman. Of those who have retired from the world it is only he who is possessed of the Five High Powers [*i.e.* magical power; divinely clear hearing; intent contemplation; calling to mind former existences; and divinely clear vision] and is master of the Eight Attainments, [*i.e.* eight stages of meditation; the first, second, third, and fourth trance; the realm of the infinity of space, the realm of the infinity of consciousness, the realm of nothingness, and the realm of neither perception nor yet non-perception] that can successfully make the wish, and no one can do so who is lacking in these excellences. Of those, even, who possess these excellences it is he, and only he, who has such firm resolve that he is ready to sacrifice his life for the Buddhas that can successfully make the wish, but no other. Of those who possess this resolve it is he, and only he, who has great zeal, determination, strenuousness, and endeavour in striving for the qualities that make a Buddha that is successful."

[2] Legge, *A Record of Buddhistic Kingdoms; being an account of the Chinese Monk Fa Hien, of his travels in India and Ceylon, in search of the Buddhist books of discipline.* Oxford: 1886, page 64. Compare also *Record of the Buddhistic Kingdoms:* translated from the Chinese by Herbert A. Giles; Shanghai, 1877, page 48.

[3] The *Purâṇas* mention this town as situated in the mythical North close to the Uttara-Kurus, the country of the Hyperboreans. Perhaps Na-pei-keâ is identical with the N â b h a k a of the Kâlsi and Shâhbâzgaṛhi versions of the XIII Rock Edict of Aśoka.

Krakucchanda Buddha. At the place where he and his father met and at that where he attained to *parinirvâṇa*, monasteries and stûpas were erected." The Chinese Buddhist pilgrim Hiuen Tsiang, who travelled through India between A. D. 629 and 645, states in his *Si-yu-ki*[1] :—"To the south of the city of Kapilavastu, going 50 *li* or so, we come to an old town where there is a stûpa. This is the place where Krakucchanda Buddha was born during the *mahâ-bhadrakalpa* [*i.e.* the present, or the age of the five sages, *viz.* Kakusandha, Koṇâgamana, Kassapa, Gautama Buddha and Metteyya], when men lived to sixty thousand [others say 40,000] years. To the south of the city, not far, there is a stûpa; this is the place where, having arrived at complete enlightenment, he met his father. To the south-east of the city is a stûpa where are that Tathâgata's relics *(of his bequeathed body)*; before it is erected a stone pillar about thirty feet high, on the top of which is carved a lion. On its side is a record relating to the circumstances of his Nirvâṇa. It was erected by Aśoka-râja." *See* also Plate I, Nos. 8 and 9.

The ruins of this large ancient city are still existing between the modern villages of Lori-kî-kudân and Goṭihvâ, about 2 miles south-west of Taulihvâ, and about 8½ miles south-west of the Śrînagar or Sirinagar Sâgar, near which stood the southern gate of Kapilavastu, *see* Plate II. The three stûpas and monasteries mentioned by Fa Hien and Hiuen Tsiang are still visible. and Krakucchanda's Nirvâṇa Stûpa, standing in the middle of the village of Goṭihvâ, still rises to a height of about eighty feet. The Buddhist origin of these ruins is quite forgotten, as the remains are ascribed by the villagers to Lori, the great *Âbhîra* or Ahîr hero. Aśoka's lion-pillar, with its edict, however, does not exist any longer above ground, and undoubtedly lies buried amongst the *débris* of the Nirvâṇa Stûpa. The three boulders worshipped as *mahâdêos*, and lying close to the relic shrine of Kakusandha Buddha, are no fragments of this pillar. About one mile east of Lori-kî-kudân, and about one and a-half mile south of Taulihvâ, near the village of Bhaṛdâwâ, rises another stûpa, on the top of which are the ruins of an old Śaiva temple, dating from the Middle Ages, with fragments of good sculpturing lying about.

Material objects of worship for the Buddhists are the relics of holy persons and the monuments erected to their memory by the piety of a grateful posterity. All such objects are *dhâtus*. distinguished into three classes: *śârîrika*, corporeal relics, *i.e.* the remains of a corpse after cremation; *uddesika*, memorials; and *pâribhogika*, objects having served the use of the Buddhas or Saints, such as sacred spots, holy trees, or a shrine, a garment, an alms-bowl, or a stick, and the like. One would expect that *dhâtus*, on account of their very nature, acquire their sacred character after the demise of the person to be commemorated, not before. The theory seems to be in accordance with this view; an exception being made with the Bodhi-trees, which are considered *chaityas*, both during the life of the Buddhas and after their demise. Bone relics of the more ancient Tathâgatas are rare. We find that all the bones of Kâśyapa Buddha (*i.e.* "swallower of light") were deposited under a stûpa at Śrâvastî, those of Krakucchanda Buddha at Kshemavatî, and of

[1] Beal, *Buddhist Records of the Western World.* Translated from the Chinese of Hiuen Tsiang. London: 1884, Volume II, page 18.

Koṇâgamana (*i.e.* "radiant with the colour of pure gold") at Śobhavatî. Much more numerous are the relics of Śâkyamuni, his Disciples, and other Saints. It is difficult to determine in what period these holy remains commenced to be religiously venerated; but there is no doubt that long before the time of Aśoka that worship was already fully developed. Relics of a nondescript kind, although not the less remarkable, because so eminently characteristic, are the shadow relics. In many places devout Buddhists were shown some cavern in which the Buddha, immediately on his reaching extinction, had left his shadow, *e.g.* near Kauśâmbî, Bodhi-Gayâ, and Nagara.

The monuments of Buddhist sacred architectural and sculptural Art have been the subject of unwearied research, and deservedly so, because they constitute a most interesting part of early Indian Archæology. The most general name for a Buddhist sanctuary is *chaitya*, a term not only applying to buildings, but to sacred trees, memorial stones, holy spots, images and religious inscriptions, hence all edifices having the character of a sacred monument are *chaityas*, but not all *chaityas* are edifices. Amongst the buildings of a sacred nature the most prominent are the *vihâra* and the *stûpa*. Vihâra designates both a monastery, or abode of the living Buddha, and a sanctuary with images. The *stûpa* (Pâli *thûpa*) is often in a loose way identified with the Dagoba, or *dhâtugarbha*. Strictly speaking, the *dhâtugarbha* is only a part of the stûpa, being the shrine in which the holy relic is deposited, the *arca* of the sanctuary. As most stûpas are erected over relics, they may be called Dagobas; still not all stûpas contain relics, many stûpas having been erected merely as monuments on the spots where some memorable events had occurred. It is more than probable, and generally admitted, that stûpas originally are grave-mounds of illustrious persons. Even the outward shape of the stûpa shows its affinity to the grave-mound; the dome answers to the *tumulus*, the railings to the fencing or circle of stones, the top or *palus* to the stake or column on the grave. The most ancient stûpas, such as are represented in the oldest sculptures of Sânchi, Bharahut, and Mathurâ, show a square or circular base, either with or without a railing. On the base is placed a dome surmounted by a graduated inverted pyramid which is connected with the dome by a short neck. The whole is surmounted by an umbrella, or a series of umbrellas one above the other; the umbrellas are hung with garlands, streamers, or flags. The Dagoba in the cave Temple at Kârle is of the same type; the oldest stûpas in Ceylon, as well as the oldest chaityas in Nepâl and the oldest stûpas and *prasâdas*, or Towers, in Burma are of the same description. It is well known that the Buddhists themselves attach a symbolic meaning to the stûpa or its parts. The two, three, five, seven, nine, and thirteen umbrellas, and the gradations of the inverted pyramid suggest divisions of the Universe. Both the Buddhists of the North and their brethren of the South see in certain stûpas representations of Mount Meru.

Passing on to Buddhist iconography, we repeat the often-made remark that images of the Buddha are wholly absent from the oldest sculptures of Sânchi, Bharahut, and Mathurâ. Even in cases where the presence of the Lord must be presupposed, it is indicated by symbols, such as footprints, a wheel, a seat or altar, above which is an umbrella with garlands. A scene on the sculptured gate of Bharahut represents

A j â t a ś a t r u, a son of S e n i y a B i m b i s â r a (who killed his father and succeeded him as king of R â j a g ṛ i h a), kneeling before the footprints of the Buddha, whereas the inscription distinctly says "A j â t a ś a t t u pays his homage to the Lord." There are many other instances which go far to prove that images of Buddha Śâkyamuni and his six last predecessors, and their being worshipped, date from a period posterior to Aśoka. If the dates found on the numerous inscriptions added to representations of Buddha Śâkyamuni, unearthed at Mathurâ, refer to the Śaka era, which is most probable, the custom of honouring the founder of the Buddhist creed by images must have been common in the beginning of the first century of our era. The holy tree of wisdom, which plays such an important part in all mythologies, is with the Buddhists a real *chaitya*. Systematically it is classed as a *pâribhogika chaitya*, but originally such trees are *uddesika*. The reverence paid by the Buddhists to the Bodhi-trees goes doubtless back to the most ancient times, and is decidedly older than the custom of setting up images.[1]

[1] *See* Kern, *l. c.*, pages 88-99.

CHAPTER III.

ŚOBHAVATÎ, THE BIRTHPLACE OF BUDDHA KOṆÂGAMANA.

ACCORDING to the canonical books of the Southern and Northern Buddhists Koṇâgamana Buddha, or Kanakamuni was born in the *mahâbhadrakalpa* at Śobhavatî, or Śubhavatî in the house of the Brâhman Yajñadatta. He is called Kanakamuni, because at the time of his birth a shower of gold (*kanaka*) is said to have fallen. Human life is supposed to have reached in his time forty or thirty thousand years, and so many persons were converted by him. Fa Hien[1] going north from Nâbhika (see Chapter II), less than a *yojana* (or about 7 miles). came to a town which had been the birthplace of Kanakamuni Buddha. At the place where he and his father met[2] and where he obtained to *parinirvâṇa* stûpas were erected. Hiuen Tsiang's description,[3] however, is more to the point. "To the north-east of the town of Krakucchanda Buddha, going about thirty *li* (about 5 miles) we come to an old capital (or great city), in which there is a stûpa. This is to commemorate the spot where in the *bhadrakalpa*, when man lived to the age of forty thousand years, Kanakamuni Buddha was born. To the north-east of the city, not far, is a stûpa; it was here, having arrived at complete enlightenment, he met his father. Further north there is a stûpa containing the relics of his bequeathed body; in front of it is a stone pillar with a lion on the top, and about 20 feet high; on this is inscribed a record of the events connected with his *Nirvâṇa;* this was built by Aśoka-râja." *See* also Plate I, Nos. 10 and 11. Fa Hien's further statement. that less than a *yojana* to the east of Koṇâgamana's Nirvâṇa-stûpa lies Kapilavastu, is quite incorrect, as the capital of the Śâkyas (see Chapter VII) is situated just five miles to the north-west of Aśoka's broken lion-pillar lying on the western bank of the Nigâlî Sâgar (Plate III).

The remains of the brick circumvallation of the ancient city Śobhavatî are still distinctly traceable near the modern hamlets of Tilaura and Gobarî about 6½ miles north-east of Lori-kî-kudân and Goṭihvâ, near which place stands Krakucchanda's Nirvâṇa-stûpa. The two stûpas, the one inside the city and the other not far to the north-east of it, are now mere low mounds of ruins, whilst the great Nirvâṇa-stûpa of Koṇâgamana, or Koṇâkamana, is, despite its great age, still fairly well-preserved, and rears its imposing pile close to Aśoka's Edict Pillar, just one mile and a-half due north-east of Tilaura Koṭ and about one mile south of the village of Niglîvâ[4] (Plate II). The lower inscribed portion of this pillar (Plate IV), which on excavation was found to measure 10 feet 6 inches in depth and at its base 8 feet 2 inches in circumference, is still fixed *in situ*, resting on a square masonry foundation, 7 feet by 7 by 1, and being embedded in the western embankment

[1] Legge, *l. c.*, page 64; Giles, *l. c.*, page 49.

[2] It seems to be necessary to have a meeting between every Buddha and his father.

[3] Beal, *l. c.*, Volume II, page 19.

[4] Niglîvâ, a small village in the Nepalese tahsîl Taulihvâ of zillah Buṭaul, is about 38 miles north-west of the Uska Bázár station on the Bengal and North-Western Railway, and eighteen miles north of Chilliâ police-station in the Basti District.

From a negative by Mr E W Smith

Photo-etching-Survey of India Offices, Calcutta, August 1897

UPPER HALF OF ASOKA'S PILLAR LYING ON WESTERN BANK OF NIGÂLÎ SÂGAR

of the lake. A short distance to the north-east, close to the brink of the water, lies the upper half of Aśoka's Edict Pillar (see Plate V), measuring 14 feet 9 inches in length and 2 feet in diameter at its uppermost and 2 feet 6 inches at its lowest end. The lion-capital is wanting, and lies unquestionably buried amongst the *débris* surrounding the lake, or possibly may rest at the bottom of the lake's water. The pillar is known far and wide to the people of the Tarâi under the name of *Bhîmasena-kî-nigâli*, or "Bhimsena's smoking pipe," and the lake as well as the neighbouring village of Niglîvâ owe their names to this popular notion. From evidences still observable it seems almost certain that this handsome column of polished sandstone was destroyed through the excessive heat of a raging forest-fire, so common in the Tarâi, between the seventh century, the date of Hiuen Tsiang's visit, and the tenth century, to which period belongs the oldest inscription[1] incised in beautiful lapidary characters of that time on about the middle of the fallen half. Just below it is engraved a pilgrim's record, dating from the latter half of the twelfth century A. D., which reads as follows: *Śrî-Tapumalla[ḥ] nityam jayatu* 1234. "Hail! May Tapumalla live long! Samvat 1234." or A. D. 1177-78. These inscriptions, being thus found about 18 feet above the original base of the pillar, could not so easily have been incised in such a high place, had the column still stood intact in its original height, which was not about 20 feet, as stated by Hiuen Tsiang, but about 28 feet.

The new edict of Aśoka (Plate IV) is incised in four beautifully engraved lines on the lower half of the mutilated lion-pillar, just ten feet six inches above its base, and has suffered by its fracture a great deal on the left side in losing the first five letters of the third as well as the first seven of the fourth line; but as fortunately a part of the wording of the Rummindei Pillar (*see* Chapter VI) agrees closely with that of the Niglîvâ Pillar, it makes the restoration of the lost portions easy and absolutely certain. The edict runs as follows:—"King Piyadasi, beloved of the gods, having been anointed fourteen years, increased for the second time the stûpa of Buddha Koṇâkamana; and having been anointed [*twenty years*], he came himself and worshipped; [*and*] he caused [*this stone pillar to be erected*]." The contents of this inscription do not agree with Hiuen Tsiang's statement "on this (pillar) is inscribed a record of the events connected with (Kanakamuni's) nirvâṇa." As Hiuen Tsiang was no epigraphist, his notices about the contents of inscriptions mentioned by him are invariably incorrect. This edict is probably the earliest archæological confirmation we have of the actual preservation, in early Buddhist times, of the memory of Koṇâgamana. The only other evidence of a similar kind is the bas-relief of Koṇâgamana's *bodhi*-tree figured at Plate XXIX of Cunningham's *Bharhut Stûpa*. The value of this edict for the early history of Buddhism has been pointed out by Hofrat Dr. Bühler[2] in a preliminary notice of the document. The edict also proves that Professor Kern[3] was right when he declared, on the strength

[1] It contains the well-known mystic formula:—*Oṃ oṃ maṇi-padume hûṃ*, "hail! hail! glory be to the jewel in the lotus," *i.e.* the Bodhisattva Padmapâṇi, so often found engraved on boulders and cliffs near the highways of Tibet and Nepâl.

[2] *Wiener Zeitschrift fur die Kunde des Morgenlandes*, Volume IX, page 175 ff; *Academy*, April 27, 1895. *See* also *Annual Progress Report* of the Archæological Survey Circle, North-Western Provinces and Oudh, for 1894-95 paragraph 3.

[3] *Geschiedenis van het Buddhisme in Indie*, Volume I, page 321.

of the evidence of the relievos at Bharahut, that the portion of the Buddhist doctrine in the *Dîgha* and *Majjhima-Nikâya*, referring to previous Buddhas, was settled in the third century B.C. Perhaps it teaches us even a little more. First, the statement of Aśoka-Piyadasi that "he increased" or enlarged the stûpa *for the second time* in the fifteenth year after his coronation as Emperor, or in the nineteenth of his reign, means that he twice restored it, adding to its size. Hence the monument must have been erected before the beginning of the king's reign, or before B.C. 259, and it must have enjoyed considerable fame and sanctity, as is also apparent from the fact that Aśoka in his twenty-fifth year personally visited and worshipped it. The dogma of the Buddhas anterior to Gautama Buddha must not only have been developed, but must also have been fixed locally, before it could occur to "the Faithful" to build or renew stûpas in honour of these Buddhas. It seems difficult to believe that all these stages of the development of the Buddhist doctrine could have been accomplished in a very short time. Secondly, according to the *Buddhavamśa* (XXIII, 29)—one of the latest books included in the Canon of the *Piṭakas*—Buddha Koṇâgamana reached *nirvâṇa, i.e.* died in the Pabbata Ârâma, that is, in the "Mountain *Plaisance* or Monastery," which suggested to Hofrat Dr. Bühler the conjecture that we have to look near the site of his Nirvâṇa-stûpa for the place of his death. The Pabbata Ârâma lies just thirteen miles north-east of Nigâlî Sâgar on the lower slopes of the Tarâi hills, overtopped by the snowclad peaks of Dhavalagiri and Muktinâth, and its deserted site is now known as Śaina-Maina (Plate II). Vast ruins of fallen monasteries and the remains of three immense wells, built of huge ancient bricks, are hidden away in dense shrubby jungle.

Such results are by no means without value for the early history of Buddhism. As the Buddhists worshipped Śâkyamuni's predecessors in the beginning of the third century B.C., or even earlier, and erected stûpas in memory of their nirvâṇa, it becomes almost certain that the origin of Buddhism lies very much earlier, and that, therefore, it is impossible, as some European scholars have done, to fix the nirvâṇa of Gautama Buddha in B. C. 350, or in B. C. 325. Thus the remoter date, circa B. C. 477, gains also on this consideration greater probability, and the attempts to reduce the distance between Śâkyamuni's death and the accession of Aśoka, against the Ceylonese canonical books, become more difficult. In addition the new edict gives us historicul facts for the 19th and 25th years of Aśoka's reign, which dates are not mentioned in the other edicts; and it shows that Aśoka's rule extended in the north-east as far as the hill frontier of Nepâl. Perhaps the Nepâlese tradition is right when it asserts that the valley, too, belonged to the Maurya Empire.

The Nigâlî Sâgar is an expansive sheet of water, being an oblong measuring about 940 feet by 440. A short distance from the western embankment of the lake, on which the mutilated portion of the edict pillar stands, are vast brick ruins stretching far away in the direction of the southern gate of Kapilavastu. Amongst the heaps of ruins, the Nirvâṇa-stûpa of Koṇâgamana is clearly discernible, the base of its hemispherical dome being about 101 feet in diameter, and its present height still about thirty feet. The dome seems to have been constructed of solid brick to a depth of about 20 feet, whilst the interior is filled up with earth-packing. This dome rests on a great circular mass, 109 feet in diameter, built in the shape of a

From a negative by Mr. E. W. Smith. Photo-etching-Survey of India Offices, Calcutta, August 1897

GENERAL VIEW OF NIGÂLÎ SÂGAR NEAR NIGLÎVÂ

huge brick drum, about six feet high, cased with solid bricks, the bricks used being of a very great size, 16 inches by 11 by 3, thus leaving a procession-path round the exterior of about eight feet in breadth. About ten feet beyond the great circular base all round was apparently a stone-railing with gateways, the positions of which can still be traced. It is thus abundantly evident that the corporeal relics of Koṇâgamana, collected from his funeral pyre, were carefully and securely interred in this stûpa, and that his Nirvâṇa-stûpa is undoubtedly one of the oldest Buddhist monuments still existing in India. On all sides around this interesting monument are ruined monasteries, fallen columns, and broken sculptures.

About one mile and a-half to the east of Nigâlî Sâgar is a deserted site, locally known by the name of Kudâi-Kôṭ (Plate II), measuring about 350 feet by 200. The interior is studded with the ruins of several small brick stûpas and heaps of broken sculpturing. In the absence of any epigraphical evidence discovered on the spot, it is impossible to say to what period these fragmentary relics of the past may belong. On topographical reasons, however, I am inclined to identify this spot with the "arrow-fountain" *(śarakûpa)* of Hiuen Tsiang (Plate I, No. 19), the more so as still close to one of the small ruined stûpas a clear spring of water, having a slightly mineral taste, gushes forth from the ground. For further details, *see* Chapter VII, page 44.

CHAPTER IV.

THE LUMBINÎ GROVE, THE BIRTHPLACE OF BUDDHA ŚÂKYAMUNI.

ACCORDING to the canonical books of the Buddhists, the pleasure garden of *sâl*-trees, called Lumbinî grove, was situated between Kapilavastu, the capital of the Śâkyas, and Devadaha (Devahrada), or Koḷi (*alias* Vyâghrapura), the capital of the Koḷyas or Koḍyas, and belonged to the inhabitants of both cities (*see* Chapter I, page 4). The name Lumbinî is, according to some Northern texts, said to have been derived from that of the queen of Suprabuddha,[1] the king of Koḷi, whose daughter was Mahâmâyâ, the mother of Gautama Buddha. Fa Hien[2] says "50 *li* (or about 8⅓ miles) east from the city (Kapilavastu) was a garden, named Lumbinî (*i.e.* "the place of liberation"), where the queen (Mahâmâyâ) entered the pond and bathed. Having come forth from the pond on the northern bank, after walking twenty paces, she lifted up her hand, laid hold of a branch of a tree, and, with her face to the east, gave birth to the heir-apparent. When he fell to the ground, he immediately walked seven paces. Two dragon-kings appeared and washed his body. At the place where they did so, there was immediately formed a well, and from it as well as from the above pond, where the queen bathed, the monks even now constantly take the water and drink it." Hiuen Tsiang,[3] whose description of the garden contains more details, travelled from the "arrow-fountain" stûpa (Plate I, No. 19) north-east about 80 or 90 *li* (or between 13⅓ and 15 miles) to the La-fa-ni, *i.e.* Lavaṇî (Lumbinî) garden. "Here is the bathing tank of the Śâkyas, the water of which is bright and clear as a mirror, and the surface covered with a mixture of flowers. To the north of this 24 or 25 paces there is an *Aśoka*-tree,[4] which is now decayed; this is the place where the Bodhisattva was born on the eighth day of the second half of the month Vaiśâkha. The school of the Sthaviras say it was on the fifteenth day of the second half of the same month. East of this is a stûpa (Plate I, No. 20) built by Aśoka-râja, where the two dragons bathed the body of the prince. When the Bodhisattva was born, he walked without assistance in the direction of the four quarters, seven paces in each direction, and said: "I am the only lord in heaven and earth; from this time forth my births are finished." Where his feet had trod there sprang up great lotus

---

[1] In Southern texts Suprabuddha is the brother of the Śâkya Daṇḍapâṇi, whose daughter Gopâ became Prince Siddhârtha's chief queen. According to Hardy, *Manual of Buddhism*, page 152, Suprabuddha's daughter was Yaśodharâ, the mother of Râhula; but (page 134) Suprabuddha is called the father of Mahâmâyâ.

When the Buddha spent the fifteenth rainy season after his enlightenment in the Bâniyan grove at Kapilavastu, he had to endure a grave insult from Suprabuddha, his father-in-law. One day as the latter was informed that the Tathâgata was about to go his begging round in a certain quarter of the town, he went out, after intoxicating himself with liquor, planted himself in the middle of the street, barring the passage to the Buddha and vilely abusing him. The Master, quietly glancing at Ânanda, his favourite disciple, uttered the prediction that in a week Suprabuddha should be swallowed alive by the earth. Suprabuddha laughed at that prediction, and imagined that he might easily avert his doom by remaining during a week in the tower of his palace; but he should experience that no place on earth can afford shelter to the perpetrator of a wicked deed [*Dhammapadam*, v. 128]. On the fatal day the earth burst open under his feet, and he sunk into the abyss down to the bottom of the Avîchi hell as a punishment for his wickedness.

[2] Legge, *l. c.*, page 67; Giles, *l. c.*, page 51.

[3] Beal, *l. c.*, Volume II, pages 24 and 25.

[4] It is curious that Hiuen Tsiang should state Prince Gautama was born under an *Aśoka*-tree (*Jonesia asoka*), whilst all canonical books inform us that the child was born under a *sâl*-tree (*Shorea robusta*).

From a negative by Bhairon Bakhsh. Photo-etching-Survey of India Offices, Calcutta, August 1897.

ASOKA'S PILLAR AT RUMMINDEI NEAR BHAGVÂNPUR

flowers. Moreover, two dragons sprang forth, and, fixed in the air, poured down the one a cold and the other a warm water stream from his mouth, to wash the prince. To the east of this stûpa are two fountains of pure water, by the side of which have been built two stûpas (Plate I, No. 21). This is the place where two dragons appeared from the earth. When the Bodhisattva was born, the attendants and household relatives hastened in every direction to find water for the use of the child. At this time two springs gurgled forth from the earth just before the queen, the one cold and the other warm, using which they bathed him. To the south of this is a stûpa (Plate I, No. 22). This is the spot where Śakra, the lord of the Dêvas, received the Bodhisattva in his arms. When the Bodhisattva was born, then Śakra, the king of Dêvas, took him and wrapped him in an exquisite and divine robe. Close to this there are four stûpas (Plate I, No. 23) to denote the place where the four heavenly kings received the Bodhisattva in their arms. When the Bodhisattva was born from the right side of his mother, the four kings wrapped him in a golden-coloured cotton vestment, and placing him on a golden slab *(bench)* and bringing him to his mother, they said, 'the queen may rejoice indeed at having given birth to such a fortunate child!' If the Dêvas rejoiced at the event, how much more should men! By the side of these stûpas and not far from them is a great stone pillar (Plate I, No. 24), on the top of which is the figure of a horse, which was built by Aśoka-râja. Afterwards, by the contrivance of a wicked dragon, it was broken off in the middle and fell to the ground. By the side of it is a little river which flows to the south-east. The people of the place call it *the river of oil.* This is the stream which the Dêvas caused to appear as a pure and glistening pool for the queen, when she brought forth her child, to wash and purify herself in, now it is changed and become a river, the stream of which is still unctuous."

At the end of November 1896 I set out on my second journey to Niglîvâ in order to meet General Khaḍga Shamsher, the Governor of Pâlpa, and to superintend the contemplated excavations around Buddha Koṇâgamana's Nirvâṇa stûpa near the banks of the Nigâli Sâgar. By a lucky chance our meeting could not take place at Niglîvâ, but instead of was arranged for near the village of Paḍêriyâ, just two miles north of the Nepâlese tahsíl-town Bhagvânpûr in zillah Buṭaul, and 13 miles south-east of Niglîvâ. Close to the General's camp, near the *débris* of four stûpas, stood a slightly mutilated pillar (Plate VI), rising about 10 feet above ground, and being covered with many records of pilgrims' visits, one of which was incised about A. D. 700. On digging away the accumulated *débris*, it proved to be an Aśoka monolith 22′-4″ high, standing upon a masonry platform, and to bear about 9′-8″ from its base a well-preserved inscription (Plate VIII, No. 3) of the Maurya period in five lines. The pillar tapers slightly, as its circumference is at the base 8′-3″, near the inscribed portion 7′-5″, and at the top 6′-6″. At an equal distance of 18 inches, all round the base of the pillar, runs a square brick railing of 5′-9″ and 2′-10″ high. The inscription fixes with absolute certainty the situation of the garden of Lumbinî, where according to the Buddhist belief Prince Siddhârtha was born. It reads as follows:—"King Piyadasi, beloved of the gods, having been anointed twenty years, came himself and worshipped saying: 'Here Buddha Śâkyamuni was born.' And he caused to be made a stone *(capital)* bearing a horse, and he caused [*this*] stone pillar to be erected. Because here the Blessed One was born, the village of Lummini has been made free of taxes and a recipient of wealth" (*see* Chapter VI). No adverse criticism can shake the evidence of the repeated assertion: "Here Buddha Śâkyamuni was born," and: "Here the Blessed One was born," as well as of the mention of Lumminigâma, which agrees with the Pâli Lumbinîgâma and the Sanskrit Lumbinîvana. This pillar, therefore, marks the identical spot which was pointed out as the birthplace of Buddha to Aśoka by the Sthavira Upagupta, the Buddhist Patriarch (*see* Chapter V). The evidence of this edict could only be set aside if it were shown that the pillar had been removed from some other place to its present position, which is an *à priori* improbable assumption; but there is collateral evidence to prove that it is still standing on its original site. We have seen above that Hiuen Tsiang, who visited the Lumbinî garden in about B. C. 636, mentions the pillar as standing close to four stûpas, the ruins of which are still visible. He further says that the pillar was originally surmounted with a horse-capital, which was afterwards sundered from it by the machinations of a wicked dragon. This exactly agrees with the facts observed by me: the capital is wanting and a small portion of the upper part of the pillar immediately below it, which actually seems to have been split off by a stroke of lightning, which the Buddhists ascribe to the anger of the Nâgas, called "dragons" by the Chinese. The horse-capital undoubtedly lies buried under the surrounding ruins, and may on excavation turn up in a well-preserved state. If Hiuen Tsiang omits to mention the inscription, the reason is no doubt that it was covered at the time of his visit by an accumulation of *débris*, and that all knowledge of its existence had been lost. As stated already, when I first saw the pillar on the 1st December 1896, only a small portion, ten feet high, was above the ground and was covered with pilgrims' records, one of which is dated about A. D. 700. This piece must, therefore, have been accessible, and the surface of the ground must have been at the present level for nearly eleven hundred years. When the excavation of the pillar was afterwards undertaken, the Aśoka record was found three feet below the surface of the soil and 9′-8″ above the base of the pillar. It is evident that the Aśoka inscription must have been covered over with rubbish at least at about A. D. 700, which circumstance explains also its present perfect state of preservation. It seems almost impossible that three feet of *débris* could have been accumulated in the sixty-four years which elapsed between the date of Hiuen Tsiang's visit and the incision of the oldest pilgrim's record at the top. Finally it may be mentioned that this deserted site is still locally called Rummindei, the first part of which name evidently represents Aśoka's Lummini and the Pâli Lumbinî. It is a curious fact that the true meaning of this ancient Buddhistic name has long been forgotten, as the present Nepâlese officials believe the word to signify the *sthân* of Rûpâ-devî. A small modern mean-looking temple, dedicated to that goddess, was about four years ago erected by a Śaiva ascetic on the top of one of the ruined stûpas, and an interesting nearly life-size stone image of Mâyâdevî, extracted from the ruins, has been set up as the tutelar deity for the worship of the purely Hindu population. The sculpture represents Mahâmâyâ in a standing position, bringing forth the infant Buddha from her right side; the child being received by the four guardian

gods of the quarters. Unfortunately the free application of oil and *sindûr* by worshippers has almost destroyed all minor details, and as the image is kept in a deep dark *cella*, it was impossible to prepare a photograph or even a drawing of it. Besides the four ruined stûpas, close to the edict pillar, there are also still the remains of the four other stûpas mentioned by Hiuen Tsiang, as well as the bathing tank of the Śâkyas and the two fountains and the well mentioned by the two Chinese pilgrims. Even "the river of oil" still flows past the ruins bearing the modern name Tillar Nadî (Plate II); the metallic lustre of whose waters gives it an oily appearance.

As the Lumbinî garden,[1] the modern Rummindei, lies just about eighteen miles to the north of Bridgmanganj station on the Bengal and North-Western Railway, the last six miles of which only are in Nepâlese territory, it is quite certain that this sacred spot will soon become again a favourite place of pilgrimage for all devout Buddhists of the world as it was of yore. For, during the last hours before the Lord's *parinirvâṇa*, whilst giving some useful counsels and instructions to Ânanda, he spoke of the four places which the pious believer ought to visit with feelings of holy reverence and awe, *viz.* the place where the Tathâgata was born [the Lumbinî Grove]; the place where he had reached perfect enlightenment [Bodhi-Gayâ]; the place where for the first time he had proclaimed the Law [the Deerpark near Benares]; and the place of his final extinction [Kusinârâ]. He dilated on the merits of pilgrimage to those places and declared: "All believers, brethren and sisters of the order, or devout men and women, who shall die while they, with believing heart, are journeying on such a pilgrimage, shall be reborn after death, when the body shall dissolve in the happy realms of heaven."[2]

The great importance of the Rummindei pillar inscription for the topography of Ancient India and the sacred history of the Buddhists has first been pointed out by the writer in an article contributed to the Allahabad *Pioneer* of the 23rd December 1896, and was later on fully discussed by Hofrat Dr. Bühler in the *Anzeiger der phil.-hist. Classe der Wiener Akademie*, January 7, 1897; *Athenæum*, March 6, 1897; and by Monsieur A. Barth in the *Journal des Savants*, February 1897, page 65 ff.

[1] Dr. L. A. Waddell's suggestion in the *Journal, Asiatic Society of Bengal*, Volume LXV, Part I, page 276, "the Lumbinî should lie a little to the north [of Koṇâgamana's pillar]" is, as we have shown above, quite incorrect and contrary to all evidence. The Lumbinî Garden lies just 13 miles south-east of Koṇâgamana's pillar, and fully 18 miles south-east of Kapilavastu.

[2] *See Mahâparinibbâna-sutta*, ed. by R. C. Childers, in the *Journal, Royal Asiatic Society*, New Series, Volume VIII, page 241; Max Müller, *Sacred Books of the East*, Volume XI, pages 90 and 91.

CHAPTER V.

AŚOKA'S PILGRIMAGE TO THE BUDDHA'S BIRTHPLACE.

THE great Emperor Aśoka, who in his Edicts calls himself Piyadasi (Priyadarśin), or Devânâm-priya "The Pious," was the son of Bindusâra and the grandson of Chandragupta, the famous founder of the Maurya dynasty. He ascended the throne in about B. C. 263; four years afterwards, at the early age of 21 years, he was anointed Emperor, and he died after an eventful reign of thirty-seven years. Aśoka is described[1] by the Buddhist chronicles as something like a monster in his youth, hence his name Kâlâśoka "The Black Aśoka," which denotes the Maurya King in his dark and sinful days, and which designation is almost synonymous with Chaṇḍâśoka, "Aśoka, the Wicked," and Kâmâśoka, "Aśoka, the Lustful," as the monarch is called before his conversion to Buddhism, which event is said to have taken place three years after his anointment (abhisheka), or in the 7th year of his reign, after which he became Dharmâśoka.[2] *i.e.*, an exemplary ruler. However, the true date of his conversion to Buddhism cannot be deduced with anything like precision. At any rate the above date assigned to it by the Ceylonese chronicles is wrong, and perhaps the result of a confusion between the monarch becoming "a pretender to the Faith" and his formal conversion as a fervent Buddhist. It is possible that the real date of Aśoka's formal conversion is eighteen years after his anointment, or twenty-two of his reign, the alleged date of the third Council at Pâṭaliputra. If we adopt the interpretation that Aśoka had been an *upâsaka*, or lay devotee, more than six years before he entered the *Samgha* or the monastic life, this will carry us to the year 28 or 29 of his reign. About that period or somewhat later he lost his queen Asandhimittâ, when he joined the Samgha, *i.e.* became a Member of the Order, or the Congregation of the Priests. Four years afterwards he left the priesthood, and re-married by raising to the dignity of queen the ill-natured Tishyarakshâ or Tishyarakshitâ. The life and deeds of Aśoka have become the subject of a series of Northern Buddhist tales, which in few points only show coincidences with the Ceylonese traditions. From a literary point of view those tales are highly remarkable, but the whole series has the character of an historical romance containing bits of genuine history mixed up with a great deal of fiction. His numerous Rock and Pillar Edicts—those invaluable documents, so precious in many respects,—afford us also no real insight into the monarch's character. They show to a certain extent that he was not devoid of vanity, and that he was much addicted to moralizing; but at the same time he seems to have been in earnest with his endeavours to heighten the moral standard of his subjects. His edicts, with a few exceptions, contain nothing particularly Buddhistic; some passages must even have been distasteful to many of his co-religionists. More than once he prides himself of his kind feelings towards all sects, of the various benefits he bestows upon all of them, and of his

[1] Kern, *l. c.*, pages 112-116.

[2] *See Divyâvadâna*, ed. by E. B. Cowell and R. A. Neil, Cambridge, 1886, pages 374, 381 ff.

the Âjîvikas (*i.e.* Vaishṇava àscetics) and
d Jaina ascetics); whereas the Buddhists in their writings,
ose an opportunity to blacken those hated rivals. The
Rock Edict and the Rûpnâth, Sahasrâm and Siddapur
, in which he gives vent to his zealotic feelings, belong to
d 34, of his reign. The traditions in various works of the
rding the last days of Aśoka's reign, tend to impress us
nce so powerful monarch, when in his old age he suffered
vas checked in his extravagances by his ministers and the Prince Regent Sampadin (or Samprati), the son of Prince Kuṇâla, and that already before his death a current of reaction had set in against his protection of Buddhism to the detriment of other communities.

According to the newly-discovered Rummindei Pillar Edict, Aśoka went on a pilgrimage to the sacred shrines of the Buddhists situated in the extreme north of his Empire twenty years after his anointment, or in the 25th year of his reign. Very probably he visited on this occasion, as the legend in the *Divyâvadâna* (page 386 ff.)[1] asserts, not only the Lumbinîvana, or the Lumbinî Grove, but also further east Kusinârâ, the site of Gautama Buddha's Parinirvâṇa, and Râmagrâma, and further west Kapilavastu, the Nirvâṇa-stûpas of Koṇâgamana and Krakucchanda and the old town of Śrâvasti, in several of which localities pillars with his inscriptions were still existing in Hiuen Tsiang's times. According to the *Divyâvadâna* Sthavira Upagupta, the fifth great teacher and Elder of the Northern Buddhist Church, was the converter and spiritual adviser of Aśoka. At the request of Yaśas, the Elder and Metropolitan of Pâṭaliputra, Aśoka invited Upagupta, who was at that time staying at Mathurâ, to come to Pâṭaliputra, and boats were provided by the Emperor for the long river journey down the Jamnâ and Ganges. On his arrival, Aśoka received him with due honours, saying: "You who resemble the Master, you who are the sole eye of the Universe, and the chief interpreter of the Sacred Law, be my refuge, Reverend Sir, and give me your commands! I shall hasten, great sage, to obey thy voice"! Upagupta replied: "O great king, the Lord, the Blessed Tathâgata, has entrusted to me as well as to you the depository of the Law. Let us make every effort to preserve that which the Leader of the World has transmitted to us, when he was in the midst of his Disciples." Then the king falling at the feet of the Sthavira Upagupta exclaimed: "This, oh Sthavira, is my desire: I wish to visit, honour, and mark by a sign for the benefit of remote posterity all the spots where the Blessed Buddha has sojourned." "Very well, oh great king," replied the Sthavira, "this thought of thine is good. I shall go this day to show you the spots where the Venerable Buddha resided." Then the Emperor equipped with a large army took perfumes, flowers, and garlands and set out in the company of the Sthavira Upagupta, who began by conducting the king to the Lumbinîvana. And extending his right hand he said to him: "Here, oh great king, the Lord (*Bhagavat*) was born; at this site, precious to behold, the first monument in honour of the Buddha should be consecrated"! The

[1] *See* also Burnouf, *Introduction à l'histoire du Buddhisme Indien*, page 382; Mons. A. Barth, in the *Journal des Savants*, February 1897, page 65 ff.; and Waddell's article *Upagupta, the Fourth Buddhist Patriarch and High Priest of Aśoka*, in *Journal, Asiatic Society of Bengal*, Volume LXVI, Part I, page 76 ff.

Emperor, after presenting one hundred thousand *suvarṇas* (gold co[illegible] of the country, raised a stûpa and retired. It would appear as if Aśok[illegible] on his Edict Pillar in the Lumbinî grove the very words *Here the Wor*[illegible] *was born,* which were uttered by Sthavira Upagupta at this sacred [illegible] remarkable coincidence seems to enhance the great value of the sem[illegible] portion of the *Divyâvadâna*.

PLATE IV.

From a negative by Mr. E. W. Smith. Photo-etching Survey of India Offices, Calcutta, August 1897.

CHAPTER VI.

THE RUMMINDEI AND NIGLÎVÂ PILLAR EDICTS OF PIYADASI, OR AŚOKA-RÂJA.

THE characters of these two new Aśoka edicts agree exactly with those of the north-eastern Pillar Edicts at Radhiâ (Ararâj), Mathiâ (Navandgaṛh), and Râmpûrvâ. Their language is the M â g a d h î of the third century B.C., which is found also in the Allahabad and Dehli Pillar Edicts, in the Kâlsî, Dhaulî and Jaugaḍa versions of the Rock Edicts, in the two Bairâṭ and the Sahasrâm Edicts, in the Cave Inscriptions of Barâbar, and in the Sôhgaurâ copper-plate, and which may be recognised by the invariable substitution of *la* for *ra*, *da* for *ḍa* and *na* for *ṇa*, by the nominative singular in *e*, and by the word *hida* for *idha*. A peculiarity, which re-occurs only in the north-eastern Pillar Edicts, is the comparatively frequent shortening of final *â* in *Piyadasina*, *lâjina*, *atana* and *kâlâpita*. New words and forms, not found in the other Aśoka Edicts, are *aṭhabhâgiye* (Rummindei, *l.* 5), *âgâcha* (R. *l.* 2; Niglîvâ *l.* 3), *ubalike* (R. *l.* 4), *usapâpite* (R. *l.* 3; N. *l.* 4), *Bhagavaṁ* (R. *l.* 4), *mahîyite* (R. *l.* 2; N. *l.* 3), and *vigaḍabhî* (R. *l.* 3), to which may be added the names of *Konâkamana* (N. *l.* 2), *Luṁminigâma* (R. *l.* 4), and *Sakyamuni* (R. *l.* 2). The wording of the two Edicts agrees very closely, and leaves no doubt that they were incised at the same time.[1]

TEXT OF THE RUMMINDEI EDICT.[2]

[1] DEVÂNA-PIYENA PIYADASINA *lâjina-vîsativasâbhisitena*
[2] *atana-âgâcha mahîyite hida*-BUDHE-*jâte* SAKYAMUNÎ-*ti*
[3] *silâ-vigaḍabhî-châ kâlâpita silâthabhe-cha usapâpite*
[4] *hida*-BHAGAVAṀ-*jâte-ti* LUṀMINIGÂME *ubalike-kaṭe*
[5] *aṭhabhâgiye-cha* [||].

TRANSLATION.

King P i y a d a s i, beloved of the gods (or dear to the gods),[3] having been anointed 20 years, came himself and worshipped saying: "Here B u d d h a Ś â k y a m u n i was born." And he caused to be made a stone *(capital)* representing a horse; and he caused *(this)* stone pillar to be erected. Because here the W o r s h i p f u l O n e was born, the village of L u ṁ m i n i has been made free of taxes and a recipient of wealth.

REMARKS.

Âgâcha stands for Pâlî *âgachcha*, Sanskṛit *âgatya*, and shows the substitution, frequent in the Prâkṛits, of a single consonant for a double one as well as the then necessary lengthening of a preceding short vowel.

---

[1] *See* Hofrat Dr. Bühler in *Epigraphia Indica*, Volume V, pages 1-6.

[2] *See* Plate VIII, No. 3. The words connected by hyphens are written continuously in the text. As regards the history and position of this pillar, *see* Chapter IV.

[3] The word *Devânâm-priya*, if taken in its etymological acceptation, means "dear to the gods;" probably, however, Aśoka attached to this compound the meaning of "harmless," or "pious." In latter times the Jains are designated as *Devânâm-priyâḥ*, which well accords with their being promoters of harmlessness *(ahiṃsâ)* to the extreme.

Mahîyite stands for *mahîyitam* "it has been worshipped" or "worship has been performed."

Ti rendered by "saying" may also be translated by "for" or "because." *Vigaḍabhî* is equivalent to the Sanskṛit *vigardabhî* "not so uncouth as an ass," *i.e.*, a horse; it is a compound adjective, qualifying *silâ*. Professor Dr. Bühler (*Epigraphia Indica*, Volume V, page 4) translates "and he caused to be made a stone (*slab*) bearing a big sun (?)" and (*l. c.*, page 5) he explains *vigaḍabhî* with the Sanskṛit *vikaṭâbhrî* and says: "A stone slab having a large representation of the sun, might have been put up in the Lumbinî garden, in order to indicate that Śâkyamuni claims to be *arkabandhu* or *âdityabandhu*, a scion of the solar race of I k s h v â k u."

Monsieur A. Barth in the *Journal des Savants*, February 1897, page 73, explains *ubalike* as equivalent to the Sanskṛit *udbalikaḥ*, and derives *aṭhabhâgiye* from *arthabhâga*. This latter explanation is supported by the *Divyâvadâna* (page 390), according to which Aśoka presented on his visit to the Lumbinî grove one hundred thousand *suvarṇas* to the people of the country. *See* Chapter V. *Udbalikaḥ* taken as a *bahuvrîhi* compound means "rich in taxes" or "with raised taxes," and taken as a *tatpurusha*, stands for "one who has left the taxes." Professor Bühler prefers to explain it by *avabalikaḥ* or *apabalikaḥ* "exempt from taxes."

TEXT OF THE NIGLÎVÂ EDICT.[1]

[1] DEVÂNAṀ-PIYENA PIYADASINA *lâjina-chodasavasâ* [*bhisi*] *tena*
[2] BUDHASA KONÂKAMANASA *thube-dutiyaṁ vaḍhite*
[3] [*Vîsativa*] *sâbhisitena-cha atana-âgâcha-mahîyite*
[4] [*Silâthabe-cha usa*] *pâpite* [||].

TRANSLATION.

King P i y a d a s i, beloved of the gods, having been anointed fourteen years, increased for the second time the stûpa of B u d d h a K o n â k a m a n a; and having been anointed [*twenty years*], he came himself and worshipped; [*and*] he caused [(*this*) *stone pillar to be erected*].

REMARKS.

With the form *Konâkamana* for Pâlî *Koṇâgamana* compare *Makâ* (Kâlsî Edict XIII, 2, *l.* 7) and *Maka* (Shâhbâzgarhî Edict XIII, *l.* 10) for the Greek *Magas*, as well as *Amtekinâ* (Girnâr Edict XIII, *l.* 8), *Aṁtikini* (Shâhbâzgarhî Edict XIII, *l.* 10), and *Aṁtekine* (Kâlsî Edict XIII, 2, *l.* 7) for the Greek *Antigenes*.

The two new Edicts tend to show that the Nepâl Tarâi formed part of Aśoka's dominions. This is indisputable if the Rummindei Edict declares that the Emperor remitted the taxes of the village of Luṁmini. But even the mere fact that Aśoka planted pillars all over the Tarâi favours the view that it was subject to his rule. For Aśoka's route from P â ṭ a l i p u t r a to the L u m b i n î G r o v e is perhaps marked by the series of pillars extending from B a k h r a near V a i s â l î (Besaṛh) through R a d h i â and M a t h i â to R â m p û r v â in the Champâran district of the Bengal Presidency, most of which were later on inscribed with the well-known Pillar Edicts.

[1] *See* Plate IV. For the history and position of this pillar edict, *see* Chapter III. The *lacunae* within brackets are restored according to the reading of the Rummindei Edict.

PLATE I

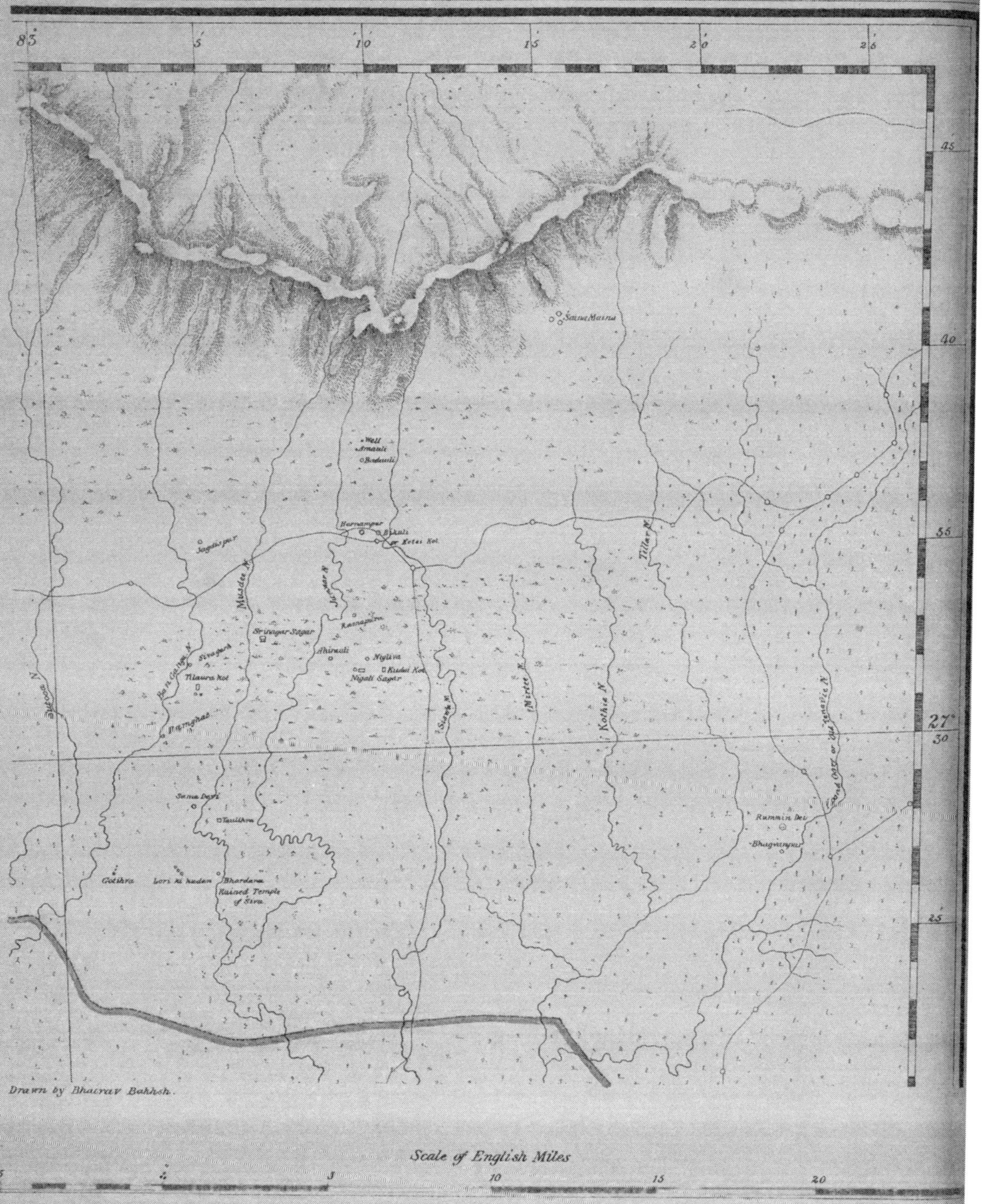

MAP OF THE PRESENT RUINS OF KAPILAVASTU IN THE NEPALESE TARAI.

Reg. No. 339, Arch. Surv., N. W. P. & Oudh.—Aug. 97.—500

Litho., S. I. O., Cal

CHAPTER VII.

KAPILAVASTU, THE CAPITAL OF THE ŚÂKYAS.

THE question as regards the correct identification of Kapilavastu, the capital city of the Śâkyas, has occupied Indian archæologists some more than forty years, and up to date only two attempts at its solution have been made. Professor Dr. Lassen, in 1858, located the ruins of Kapilavastu, on geographical calculations, at a short distance to the north-west of Gorakhpûr on the banks of the modern Rohin Nadî, which he identified with the ancient Rohiṇî; compare his *Indische Altertumskunde*, Leipzig, 1858, Volume III, page 201. To almost the same conclusions came independently Monsieur Stanislaus Julien in his *Voyages des Pèlerins Bouddhistes*, Volume III, page 356. The late Director of the Archæological Survey Department, General Sir A. Cunningham, in 1863, believed to have discovered by epigraphical evidence[1] the identity of Sâvatthi, or Śrâvastî, the capital city of the Kosalas, with the deserted site known as Sêṭ-Mahêṭ near Balrâmpûr in the Gonda district of Oudh. This identification enabled him to define also the position of Kapilavastu. As, according to the two Chinese Buddhists Fa Hien and Hiuen Tsiang, Kapilavastu lay south-east of Śrâvastî at a distance of about 80 miles, Sir A. Cunningham believed to recognize the town, for whose name he accepted the variant Kapilanagara, in the modern Nagar Khâs in the Basti District, about 81 miles south-east of Sêṭ-Mahêṭ. He published this identification in his *Ancient Geography of India*, page 414, without himself even having visited the place. Later on his Assistant, Mr. A. C. Carlleyle, who explored the districts of Basti and Gorakhpûr in the camping season of 1875-76, took up again the investigation, and as he could not find in Nagar Khâs and its neighbourhood any traces of the magnificent monuments mentioned by the Chinese pilgrims, he looked for Kapilavastu 18 miles further north amongst the remains at Bhuilâ Tâl, a place studded with brick mounds and situated on the banks of the Rawai Nadî. Although Mr. Carlleyle's expositions in the *Archæological Survey Reports*, Volume XII, pages 83-215, and Volume XXII, page 1, *ff.*, are full of unscientific deductions and devoid of critical acumen, and although his excavations on the spot did not bring to light either inscriptions or sculptures which could support the identification, Sir A. Cunningham, notwithstanding, after a short examination of the site, expressed his most perfect conviction of the accuracy of Mr. Carlleyle's identification (*see l. c.* Volume XII, pages III-IV; Volume XXII, page III). Nevertheless, that identification rested on no substantial grounds, and, in 1889,

[1] *Archæological Survey Reports*, Volume I, page 359. Mr. V. A. Smith, I. C. S., in his interesting Memorandum on *The Remains near Kasia in the Gorakhpur District*, Allahabad, 1896, page 4, greatly doubts the correctness of the hitherto accepted identification of the site of Śrâvastî, and is inclined to identify it with Chârdâ or Chahârdâh in the Bahraich District, about forty miles north-west of Sêṭ-Mahêṭ. A brief description of the ruins at Chârdâ is given in the *Monumental Antiquities and Inscriptions of the North-Western Provinces and Oudh*, Allahabad, 1891, page 293. Mr. V. A. Smith thinks that Sêṭ-Mahêṭ will probably prove to be the ancient Setabyâ, which was situated eastwards from Śrâvastî. I have, however, reliable information which tends to prove that the ruins of Śrâvastî are to be found in the Nepâl Tarâi, on the left bank of the Râptî, the ancient Achiravatî, close to the modern village of Materiyâ, just 15 miles north-east of Chârdâ. The two monoliths of Aśoka, erected in front of the Jetavana monastery in Anâthapiṇḍika's Park, are said to be still *in situ*, which information I hope to verify in the winter season of 1897-98.

was shown by me[1] to be erroneous on topographical and other reasons. The errors of Lassen, Julien, Cunningham and Carlleyle have been caused by the vague statements of the Chinese pilgrims, who both say that in travelling from Śrâvastî to Kapilavastu they went south-east. As Sir A. Cunningham had identified Śrâvastî with Sêṭ-Mahêṭ, it was but natural for him to infer that Kapilavastu must lie either in the Basti or Gorakhpur district. The country of the Śâkyas has thus by all been looked for too far south, as the town lay actually much further north. It may also be pointed out that its real position, eighteen miles north-west of the Lumbinî garden, agrees with the hints given in the Ceylonese canonical books. According to the *Ambaṭṭha-sutta* of the *Dîgha-nikâya* (III, 1, 15),[2] the banished sons of Ikshvâku or Okkâka, the ancient seer-king, settled *yatha Himavantapassê pòkharaṇiyâ tîrê mahâsâkasaṇḍô, i.e.* "where there was a great grove of *śâka*[3] trees on the bank of a lake *(situated)* on the lower slopes of the Himâlaya." This description fits the present ruins near the Śrînagar Sâgar in the Nepâlese Tarâi much better than the absolutely flat districts of Basti or Gorakhpur, which are still a great distance from the hills.

According to the canonical books of the Southern Buddhists, Kapilavatthu (Kapilavastu), or Kapilapura was situated on the banks of the Rohaṇî or Rohitâ, whilst the *Divyâvadâna* (ed. Cowell) page 348, locates the town on those of the Bhâgîrathî (*i.e.* Ganges), not far from the hermitage of Ṛishi Kapila. It is also narrated (*Jâtaka*, Volume V, page 412; *Theragâthâ*, *v.* 529,) that the river flowed between the capital of the Śâkyas and Devahrada, the capital of the Koḷyas. For, a short time before the death of king Śuddhodana there arose a dispute between the Śâkyas and Koḷyas about the water of the river Rohaṇî, which owing to an unusual drought was not sufficient to irrigate the rice-fields on both sides of the river. The quarrel rose high, and a battle would have ensued had not the Buddha, perceiving by his divine eye what was going on, hastened from Vaiśâlî through the sky to the place where the parties stood ready to fight, and moved them to lay down their arms. The eloquent discourse which he delivered on that occasion had the desired effect that he made numerous converts. Accordingly, the ruins of Kapilavastu ought to have been discovered on the western bank of the river, and the Lumbinî garden to the east of it. This is actually the case, if we identify the modern Jamuâr Nadî (Plate II) with the ancient river Rohaṇî; for the vast ruins of Kapilavastu lie on its western bank,[4] whilst the Lumbinî garden, the modern Rummindei, is just to the south-east of it.

In an old Buddhist dialogue Kapilavastu is described as a prosperous, flourishing town, and well provided with food, whose narrow streets are thronging with elephants, carriages, horses and people. "The capital was neither by day nor night without the ten noises, *viz.* the noise of elephants, the noise of horses, the noise of chariots, the noise of drums, the noise of tabours, the noise of lutes, the noise of song,

[1] *The Sharqi Architecture of Jaunpur; with Notes on Zafarabad, Sahet-Mahet, and other places in the North-Western Provinces and Oudh*, Calcutta, 1889, page 69; *see* also *Monumental Antiquities and Inscriptions in the North-Western Provinces and Oudh*, Allahabad, 1891, page 222.

[2] Edited by Rhys David and E. Carpenter, Volume I, page 92. Compare also *Suttanipâta*, *v.* 432.

[3] The *sâka*, or modern *sâkhû* is the well-known timber tree *(Tectona grandis)*, which still abounds in the forests surrounding the present ruins of Kapilavastu.

[4] By an oversight, the draftsman has shown the river Rohaṇî (Plate I) as flowing past the western side of Kapilavastu instead of past its eastern face.

the noise of cymbals, the noise of gongs, and the tenth noise of people crying: *eat ye and drink!*" An old poem in the *Sutta-nipâta* (*v.* 1012) describes the route taken by some wandering Brâhman ascetics, who travel from Kosambî to Sâketa, thence to Sâvatthi, Setabyâ, Kapilavatthu, further to Kusinârâ, Pâvâ, and Veśâli. The *Ambattha-sutta* further mentions the disinclination of the Śâkyas to show hospitality to the Brâhman ascetics who came to their settlement from Śrâvastî or other parts of India. That Kapilavastu is not mentioned in the great epic literature of the Brâhmans is easily to be accounted for, as the scenes represented in the *Mahâbhârata* and *Râmâyaṇa* mostly take place in the western parts of the peninsula, there being no need for references to the eastern portions of the country, and as Kapilavastu had already been razed to the ground during the lifetime of the Buddha. Notwithstanding all these important evidences, Monsieur E. Senart[1] still doubts the very existence of Kapilavastu and sees in it but *la ville, la forteresse de l'atmosphère*. The name of Kapilavastu evidently signifies "the tawny coloured town," being situated on the Rohaṇî, or "the red river." As a curious fact it may here be mentioned that the whole surface of the soil, surrounding the present ruins of this ancient city, is of a reddish yellow colour produced by deep deposits of carbonate of iron in the upper strata. Its etymological derivation can, therefore, not be the town of the Ṛishi Kapila,[2] the celebrated founder of the Sâṅkhya philosophy, which, moreover, was Kapilasthâna, the modern Hardwâr on the Ganges.

It would appear from the oldest texts that the country of the Śâkyas was after all only a petty Râjput State, measuring about eighty miles in length and about forty in breadth, and covering thus an area of about 2,400 miles well suited for rice cultivation,[3] and that the Buddha's father was rather a feudal baron or chieftain of a small clan, than an actual king. It is only the newer tradition that extols the power and wealth which the Buddha gave up on renouncing worldly ties. To the east their country was separated by the Rohaṇî river from that of the Koḷyas; to the west and the south their rule extended almost as far as the Aciravatî, the modern Râptî, their neighbours being the powerful Kosalas of Śrâvastî; in the north they occupied the fertile and well-wooded slopes of the present Nepâlese Sub-Himâlayas. Besides Kapilavastu, the canonical books mention the following towns and villages as situated amongst the Śâkyas or Sakkas:—Châtumâ (*Majjhima-nikâya, sutta* 67), the market-town Khomadussa (*Saṁyutta-nikâya*, ed. by Léon Feer, Volume I, page 184), Meṭalupa (*Dhamma-chetiyasuttanta, Majjhima-nikâya*), Sâmagâma (*Sutta* 104, *Majjhima-nikâya*), Saṅsumâra (Ceylonese and Burmese accounts), and Uḷumpa (Buddhaghosha's Commentary to the *Dhammapada*, page 222). At the present state of our knowledge of the Tarâi it is almost impossible to identify these localities with any certainty; although the modern Sâma Devî, about 1½ miles north-west of Taulihvâ (Plate II), may eventually turn out to be the ancient Sâmagâma. The canonical books of the

[1] *Essai sur la légende de Buddha*, 2 ième édition, Paris, 1882, page 413.

[2] Weber, *Indische Literaturgeschichte*, 2nd ed., page 303.

[3] The names of King Śuddhodana, "Pure-rice," and his four brothers, "Clear-rice," "Strong-rice," "White-rice," and "Immeasurable-rice," show the importance of this cultivation to the Śâkyas, *see* Oldenburg, *Buddha*, page 97, note.

various sects amongst the Southern as well as the Northern Buddhists speak of the great opulence of the country and mention the immense hoards of gold which the royal family and the nobility of the land had amassed. The pride and haughtiness of the Śâkyas or Sakkas was proverbial amongst the neighbouring people, and the Brâhman pilgrims, who occasionally visited their capiṭal, had to tell many a bitter tale of their scornful behaviour towards them. The fact that the Śâkyas were real forest and hill Râjputs is not without importance for their history and the explanation of their strange un-Âryan customs. It makes their assertion that their ancestors were forcibly ejected from the more civilized regions in the South very credible, though the truth of the cause of their banishment, as stated in the *Ambaṭṭha-sutta*, may be doubted. Further, their isolation in the forests may have led, as the sacred books allege, to their custom of endogamy, so repugnant to all Râjputs and to all the higher castes in India. And this custom, not their pride of race, as they themselves asserted, was no doubt the reason why the other royal families of Northern India did not intermarry with them. This isolation and the consequent estrangement from the rest of the Hindû population probably accounts also for their disinclination to show hospitality to the wandering Brâhman ascetics, who in the course of their pilgrimages came to their country. Their religion, however, seems to have been the ordinary type of Śaivism. Hiuen Tsiang, as will be stated hereafter, was still shown near the eastern gate of Kapilavastu, the old temple of Îśvara (Plate I, No. 17), where the infant Siddhârtha was taken by his father, because "the Śâkya children, who here seek divine protection, always obtain what they ask." According to the legend, the stone image raised itself and saluted the Prince. Mr. Beal (*Si-yu-ki*, Volume II, page 23, Note 59), has correctly recognized that the scene is represented on the Amarâvatî stûpa in Fergusson's *Tree and Serpent Worship*, Plate LXIX. The legend is therefore ancient, and points to the conclusion that Śiva was the *kuladevatâ* of the Śâkyas.

A few years before the *parinirvâṇa* of the Buddha, the Śâkya clan met with a sad fate. King Pasenadi, or Prasenajit, of Kosala had a son Viḍûḍabha (also called Virûḍhaka), by Vâsabhakkhattiyâ, the natural daughter of Mahânâman, the successor of Śuddhodana in Kapilavastu, and of a slave girl. It was by deceit that Vâsabhakkhattiyâ had been affianced by the Śâkyas. When the trick afterwards was discovered, and Viḍûḍabha had been slighted by the Śâkyas, he resolved to take revenge. With the assistance of the Commander-in-Chief, Dîgha-Kârâyana (or Dîrgha-Chârâyaṇa) he dethroned his father Prasenajit, who fled from Śrâvastî and died soon afterwards. Viḍûḍabha marched against Kapilavastu and on his way found the Buddha seated under an old withered *śâka*-tree. It afforded him no shade; but he told Viḍûḍabha that "the thought of the danger of his relatives and kindred made it shady." The king was moved to sympathy for the time, and went back to Śrâvastî; but the destruction of Kapilavastu was only postponed for a short space, and the Buddha acknowledged it to be inevitable in the connection of cause and effect. Shortly afterwards, Viḍûḍabha resumed the campaign, in consequence of which Kapilavastu is said to have been totally destroyed and the whole Śâkya clan exterminated. This extirpation of the whole clan can, however, not have been of much importance, as only a short time later on we find the Śâkyas of Kapilavastu putting forward a claim for obtaining the possession of a portion of the relics collected from the funeral pile of the Lord near the shrine M a k u t a-b a n d h a n a at Kusinârâ.

The Chinese pilgrim Fa Hien,[1] who visited Kapilavastu about A. D. 406, gives us the following meagre, though interesting, description of its ruins:—"Less than a *yojana* to the east[2] from this (*i e.* Buddha Koṇâgamana's Nirvâṇa-Stûpa) brought the travellers to the city of Kapilavastu (*i.e.* 'the city of beautiful virtue'); but in it there was neither king nor people. All was mound and desolation. Of inhabitants there were only some monks and a score or two of families of common people. At the spot where stood the old palace of king Śuddhodana (*i.e.* "the king white and pure,") there have been made images of the Prince and his mother; and at the places where that son appeared mounted on a white elephant when he entered his mother's womb, and where he turned his carriage round on seeing the sick man after he had gone out of the city by the eastern gate [Plate I, No. 4], stûpas [read *vihâras*] have been erected. The places *(were also pointed out)* where *(the ṛishi)* Â-e, (*i.e.* A s i t a), inspected the marks *(of Buddhaship on the body)* of the heir-apparent *(when an infant)*; where, when he was in company with N a n d a and others, on the elephant being struck down and drawn on one side, he tossed it away [Plate I, No. 1]; where he shot an arrow to the south-east, and it went a distance of thirty *li*, then entering the ground and making a spring to come forth [Plate I, No. 19], which men subsequently fashioned into a well from which travellers might drink; where after he had attained to enlightenment, Buddha returned and saw the king, his father [Plate I, No. 15]; where five hundred Śâkyas quitted their families and did reverence to Upâli,[3] while the earth shook and moved in six different ways; where Buddha preached his Law to the Devas, and the four Deva kings and others kept the four doors *(of the hall)*, so that *(even)* the king, his father, could not enter; where Buddha sat under a *nyagrodha*-tree [*Ficus indica*], which is still standing, with his face to the east, and *(his aunt)* M a h â - p r a j â p a t î presented him with a *saṅghâṭi*;[4] and *(where)* king V a i d û r y a [Viḍûḍabha or Virûḍhaka] slew the seed of Śâkya, and they all in dying became *śrota-âpannas*.[5] A stûpa[6] was erected at this last place, which is still existing.

"Several *li* north-east from the city was the king's field, where the heir apparent sat under a tree and looked at the ploughers [Plate I, No. 12].

"The country of Kapilavastu is a great scene of empty desolation. The inhabitants are few and far between. On the roads people have to be on their guard against white elephants and lions, and should not travel incautiously."

---

[1] Legge, *l. c.*, pages 64-67; Giles, *l. c.*, pages 49-50.

[2] This direction is incorrect, as Kapilavastu lies between five and six miles north-west of Aśoka's monolith, *see* Chapter III.

[3] Upâli was a *śûdra* by birth and by profession a barber, before his conversion to Buddhism; thus from the first did Buddhism assert its superiority to the conditions of rank and caste. Upâli was distinguished by his knowledge of the rules of discipline and praised on that account by the Buddha. He was one of three leaders of the first general council held at Râjagṛiha shortly after the demise of the Master, and the principal compiler of the *Vinayapiṭakam*.

[4] A *saṅghâti* is a kind of cloak, the double or composite robe of a monk, reaching from the shoulders to the knees and being fastened round the waist.

[5] The *śrota-âpanna* is he who has entered the first stage on the road towards deliverance, or Nirvâṇa. He has got rid of the first three bonds of human passion, and the doors of the states of punishment are shut for him.

[6] This stûpa, commemorating the slaughter of the 500 Śâkya maidens, who had refused to take their place in king Viḍûḍabha's harem, was at S r â v a s t î, and not at Kapilavastu; compare Hiuen Tsiang's *Si-yu-ki*, Volume II, page 11.

Hiuen Tsiang,[1] who visited Kapilavastu about A. D. 636, is as usual more communicative in his account of that place. "The country is about 4,000 *li* [or about 666⅔ miles] in circuit. There are some ten desert cities [apparently the villages and towns mentioned *supra*] in this country, wholly desolate and ruined. The capital is overthrown and in ruins. Its circuit cannot be accurately measured. The royal precincts [*i.e.* the fortified interior city, *see* Plate I] within the [exterior] city measure some 14 or 15 *li* round. They were all built of brick. The foundation walls are still strong and high. It has been long deserted. The inhabited suburbs or streets are few and waste. There is no supreme ruler: each of the towns appoints its own ruler. The ground is rich and fertile, and is cultivated according to the regular season. The climate is uniform, the manners of the people soft and obliging.

"There are a thousand or more ruined *saṅghârâmas* (monasteries) remaining; by the side of the royal precincts there is still a *saṅghârâma* with about 3,000 (read 30) followers in it, who study the Little Vehicle [*Hînayâna*] of the *Sammatiya* school. There are a couple of Deva temples, in which various sectaries worship. Within the royal precincts are some ruined foundation walls; these are the remains of the principal palace of Śuddhodana-râja; above it is built a *Vihâra* in which is a statue of the king. Not far from this is a ruined foundation, which represents the sleeping palace of Mahâmâyâ, the queen. Above this they have erected a *Vihâra* in which is a figure of the queen. By the side of this is a *Vihâra;* this is where the Bodhisattva descended spiritually into the womb of his mother. There is a representation of this scene drawn in the *Vihâra*. The *Mahâsthavira* school say that the Bodhisattva was conceived on the 30th night of the month *Uttarâshâḍha*. The other schools fix the event on the 23rd day of the same month. To the north-east of the palace of the spiritual conception is a *stûpa;* this is the place where Asita, the *rishi,* prognosticated the fortune of the royal prince.

"At the south gate of the city is a *stûpa* (Plate I, No. 1). This is where the royal prince, when contending with the Śâkya princes, cast the elephant away. The royal prince, having contended in the public competitions *(of arts and athletic exercises)* was left entirely without compeer in every exercise [Plate I, No. 18]. And now the Mahârâja Śuddhodana, after congratulating him, was about to go back to the city. At this time the coachman was leading out the elephant and just about to leave the city. Devadatta,[2] confident as ever in his brute strength, was just entering the gate from without; forthwith he asked the coachman, 'who is going to ride on this gaily caparisoned elephant?' He said, 'the royal prince is just about to return, therefore I am going to meet him.' Devadatta in an excited manner pulled the elephant down, and struck his forehead and kicked his belly, and left him lying senseless, blocking the way so that no one could pass. As they could not move him out of the way, the passers-by were stopped on their route. Nanda[3] coming

[1] Beal, *l. c.*, Volume II, pages 13-24.

[2] Devadatta is in Pâli texts the brother of Yaśodharâ, hence Siddhârtha's brother-in-law. He became, however, the deadly enemy of Buddha Śâkyamuni, whose growing fame and influence filled him with jealousy. He had become so in an earlier state of existence, and the hatred continued in every successive birth through which they reappeared in the world. The elephant had been presented to Prince Siddhârtha by the Licchavis of Vaiśâlî, and was killed by Devadatta, out of envy, with the blow of his fist.

[3] Nanda was Gautama Buddha's younger half-brother, his mother being Mahâprajâpatî.

afterwards, asked, 'who has killed the elephant?' They said, 'it was Devadatta.' Forthwith Nanda drew it on one side of the road. The prince-royal then coming, again asked, 'who had done the foul deed of killing the elephant?' They replied, "Devadatta killed it and blocked up the gate with it, and Nanda drew it on one side to clear the road." The royal prince then lifted the elephant on high and threw it across the city moat; the elephant falling on the ground caused a deep and wide ditch; the people since then have commonly called it 'the fallen-elephant ditch' [*hastigarta*].

"By the side of this [*i.e.* the elephant-throwing stûpa] is a *vihâra* in which is a figure of the royal prince. By the side of this again is a *Vihâra* [Plate I, No. 2]; this was the sleeping apartment of the queen and the prince; in it is a likeness of Yośodharâ and *(the child)* Râhula. By the side of the queen's chamber is a *vihâra* with a figure of a pupil receiving his lessons; this indicates the old foundation of the school-house of the royal prince. At the south-east angle of the city is a *vihâra* [Plate I, No. 3] in which is the figure of the royal prince riding a white and high-prancing horse; this was the place where he left the city. Outside each of the four gates of the city there is a *vihâra* [Plate I, Nos. 4-7], in which there are respectively figures of an old man, a diseased man, a dead man, and a *śramaṇa*. It was in these places the royal prince, on going his rounds, beheld the various indications, on which he received an increase of *(religious)* feeling, and deeper disgust at the world and its pleasures; and filled with this conviction, he ordered his coachman to return and go home again.

"To the north-east of the city about 40 *li* is a *stûpa* [Plate I, No. 12]. This is the spot where the prince sat in the shade of a tree to watch the ploughing festival. Here he engaged in profound meditation and reached the condition of 'absence of desire.' The king seeing the prince in the shade of the tree and engrossed in quiet contemplation, and observing that whilst the sun's rays shed their bright light around him, yet the shadow of the tree did not move, his heart, recognising the spiritual character of the prince, was deeply reverent.

"To the north-west of the capital there are several hundreds and thousands of stûpas [Plate I, No. 13], indicating the spot where the members of the Śâkya tribe were slaughtered. Virûḍhaka-râja having subdued the Śâkyas, and captured the members of their tribe to the number of 9,990 myriads [!] of people, then ordered them to be slaughtered.[1] They piled their bodies like straw, and their blood was collected in lakes. The Devas moved the hearts of men to collect their bones and bury them.

"To the south-west of the place of massacre are four little stûpas [Plate I, No. 14]. This is the place where the four Śâkyas withstood an army. When first Prasenajit became king, he sought an alliance by marriage with the Śâkya race. The Śâkyas despised him as not of their [holy] family, and so deceived him by giving him as a wife a child of a servant, whom they largely endowed. Prasenjit-râja established her as his principal queen, and she brought forth in due time a son, who

[1] The *Jâtaka* (Volume IV, page 144) relates that Viḍûḍabha, as a just punishment for his crime, miserably perished, along with his Kosala army, by a sudden flood. Hiuen Tsiang, however, says *(Si-yu-ki,* Volume II, page 12), that the king after his return to Śrâvastî went down bodily into hell in the middle of a lake.

was called Virûḍhaka-râja. And now Virûḍhaka was desirous to go to the family of his maternal uncles to pursue his studies under their direction. Having come to the south part of the city, he there saw a new preaching-hall, and there he stopped his chariot. The Śâkyas hearing of it, forthwith drove him away, saying 'how dare you, base-born fellow! occupy this abode, an abode built by the Śâkyas, intended for an abode of the Buddha?' After Virûḍhaka had succeeded to the throne, he longed to revenge his former insult; he therefore raised an army and occupied this place with his troops, who took possession of the fields. Four men of the Śâkyas who were engaged in ploughing between the rills dividing the fields, immediately opposed the progress of the soldiers, and, having scattered them, entered the town. Their clansmen, considering that their tribe was one in which there had been a long succession of universal monarchs, and that the honourable children of such righteous kings[1] had dared to act cruelly and impetuously, and without patience to kill and slay, and so had brought disgrace on their family, drove them away from their home. The four men, having been banished, went to the north among the Snowy Mountains; one became king of the country of Bâmiyân [in Afghanistân], one of Udyâna, or Ujjâna, one of Himatala [Badakshân], and one of Śâmbî. They have transmitted their kingly authority from generation to generation without any interruption.

"To the south of the city three or four *li* is a grove of *nyagrodha*-trees, in which is a *stûpa* built by Aśoka-râja [Plate I, No. 15]. This is the place where Śâkya Tathâgata, having returned to his country after his enlightenment, met his father and preached the Law. Śuddhodana-râja, knowing that the Tathâgata had defeated Mâra and was engaged in travelling about, leading people to the truth and converting them, was moved by a strong desire to see him, and considered how he could pay the reverence due to him. He therefore sent a messenger to invite the Tathâgata, saying 'formerly you promised, when you had completed your purpose to become a Buddha, to return to your native place. These are your words still unperformed; now then is the time for you to condescend to visit me.' The messenger having come to the place where the Buddha was, expressed to him the king's desire. The Tathâgata in reply said, 'after seven days I shall return to my native place.' The messenger, returning, acquainted the king with the news, on which Śuddhodana-râja ordered his subjects to prepare the way by watering and sweeping it, and to adorn the road with incense and flowers; and then, accompanied by his officers of state, he proceeded 40 *li* [about $6\frac{2}{3}$ miles] beyond the city, and there drew up his chariot to await his arrival. Then the Tathâgata with a great multitude advanced; the eight *Vajrapâṇis* surrounded him as an escort, the four heavenly kings went before him; divine Śakra with a multitude of Devas belonging to the world of desires *(kâmaloka)* took their place on the left hand; Brahmâ-râja with the Devas of the *rûpaloka* ['the region of form,' the second region of the cosmical system of the Buddhists; the lowest being the region of Kâma, or sensual pleasure] accompanied him on the right. The *bhikshu* priests walked in order behind; the Buddha by himself, as the full moon among the stars, stood in the midst; his supreme spiritual presence shook the three worlds, the brightness of his

[1] The idea is that Śâkya children, descended from holy kings, ought not to have resisted even an invader.

person exceeded that of the seven lights [the sun, moon and five planets]; and thus traversing the air he approached his native country. The king and ministers having reverenced him, again returned to the city, and they located themselves in this *nyagrodha* grove.

"By the side of the *saṅghârâma*, and not far from it, is a *stûpa;* this is the spot where the Tathâgata sat beneath a great tree with his face to the east and received from his aunt [Mahâprajâpatî[1]] a golden-tissued *kâshâya*[2] garment. A little farther on is another *stûpa:* this is the place where Tathâgata converted six princes [Anuruddha, Bhaddiya, Ânanda, Bhagu, Kimbila, and Devadatta] and five hundred Śâkyas.

"Within the eastern gate of the city, on the left of the road, is a *stûpa* [Plate I, No. 16]; this is where Prince Siddhârtha practiced *(athletic sports and competitive)* arts.

"Outside the gate is the temple of Îśvara-deva [Plate I, No. 17]. In the temple is a figure of the Deva made of stone, which has the appearance of rising in a bent position. This is the temple which the royal prince when an infant *(in swaddling clothes)* entered. King Śuddhodana was returning from the Lumbinî garden after having gone to meet the prince. Passing by this temple the king said 'this temple is noted for its many spiritual exhibitions *(miracles)*. The Śâkya children who here seek divine protection always obtain what they ask: we must take the royal prince to this place and offer up our worship.' At this time the nurse *(foster-mother)*, carrying the child in her arms, entered the temple; then the stone image raised itself and saluted the prince. When the prince left, the image again seated itself.

"Outside the south gate of the city, on the left of the road, is a *stûpa* [Plate I, No. 18]; it was here the royal prince contended with the Śâkyas in athletic sports *(arts)* and pierced with his arrows the iron targets.

"From this thirty *li* south-east is a small *stûpa* [Plate I, No. 19]. Here there is a fountain, the waters of which are as clear as a mirror. Here it was, during the athletic contest, that the arrow of the prince, after penetrating the targets, fell and buried itself up to the feather in the ground, causing a clear spring of water to flow

---

[1] Shortly after the death of king Suddhodana, the Buddha's aunt and step-mother Mahâprajâpatî Gautamî desired to forsake the world and embrace a religious life. Therefore she went to the Lord, who was then sojourning in the Bâniyân grove at Kapilavastu, and asked to become a nun. But the Buddha refused, because he would not admit females into the order, and returned to Vaisâlî. Far from giving up her design, the widowed Queen and many other Śâkya ladies cut off their hair, put on yellow garments and went on foot to Vaisâlî. When these ladies, with swollen feet and covered with dust, sorrowful, sad and tearful, stood weeping outside in the entrance porch of the Kûṭâgâra hall, they were seen by Ânanda [the body-servant and favourite disciple of Buddha Gautama], who, having ascertained the object of their journey, went to the Master and pleaded in their favour. At first the Buddha was unwilling to admit women into the congregation; at last, however, at the entreaties of Ânanda, who remembered him of the motherly care of Mahâprajâpatî, he gave his consent, but on the condition that she should accept eight weighty regulations *(garudhamma)*. Mahâprajâpatî gladly promised to accept these eight weighty regulations, not to be transgressed as long as life shall last; whereupon she with all the other Śâkya ladies became nuns. Although the Master had acceded to the wishes of Ânanda, he was fully aware of the dangerous consequences attending on the institution of the Order of Nuns. "If, Ânanda, women had not retired from household life to the houseless one, under the Doctrine and Discipline announced by the Tathâgata, religion would long endure; a thousand years would the good Doctrine abide. But since women have now retired from household life, not long will religion endure; but five hundred years will the good Doctrine abide. Just as, Ânanda, those families which consist of many women and few men are easily overcome by burglars, in exactly the same way, when women retire from household life to the houseless one, under a doctrine and discipline, that religion does not long endure. And just as, Ânanda, to a large lake a man would prudently build a dike, in order that the water might not transgress its bounds, in exactly the same way, Ânanda, have I prudently laid down eight weighty regulations not to be transgressed as long as life shall last." His misgiving proved true by the subsequent events: the ladies, even Mahâprajâpatî, were now and then fretful and some time afterwards, when the Lord sojourned at Śrâvastî, some nuns moved the indignation of the public by their scandalous behaviour. See Cullavagga X, 1—27 (ed. H. Oldenberg), Vinayapiṭaka, Volume II, London, 1880.

[2] The *kâshâya*, or reddish yellow garment, is the *saṅghâṭi*, a kind of cloak, which is folded many times and thrown over the left shoulder, the two ends hanging down before and behind.

forth. Common tradition has called this the arrow-fountain *(śarakûpa);* persons who are sick, by drinking the water of this spring are mostly restored to health; and so people coming from a distance taking back with them some of the mud *(moist earth)* of this place, and applying it to the part where they suffer pain, mostly recover from their ailments."

The discovery of the Aśoka Edict Pillar in the Lumbinî grove at Rummindei enabled me to fix also, with absolute certainty, the site of Kapilavastu and of the sanctuaries in its neighbourhood. Thanks to the exact notes left by the two Chinese travellers, I discovered its extensive ruins about eighteen miles north-west of the Lumbinî Pillar, and about six miles north-west of the Nigâlî Sâgar (Plate II), stretching between lat. 27°32′-38′ N. and long. 38°3′-10′ E. in the middle of a dense *sâl* forest over a length of about seven miles from the villages of Amauli, Baidaulî, Harnâmpûr, and Bikuli (north-east) to Śivagarḥ, Tilaurakoṭ, and Râmghâṭ on the Bangangâ (south-west), and over a breadth of about three to four miles from the villages of Râmapura, Ahiraulî, and Śrînagar on the south to the villages of Jagdîspûr and Nagrâvah on the north. The whole site is at present as dreary and desolate as when seen by Fa Hian and Hiuen Tsiang; yet every sacred spot mentioned by the two pilgrims can be easily identified. The discovery of this interesting site, therefore, opens out a very wide field indeed to the Indian archæologist, and cannot but yield the richest results in the near future. The first step to be taken by the Department will be to excavate next cold weather the most important ruins that can be absolutely identified. Special attention will be paid to the Śaiva temple on the eastern face of the old city, the ruins of which are near Bikulî close to the Kotahî Kôṭ, which certainly must be one of the oldest Śaiva monuments of which we have knowledge, and which possesses great interest for the history of the Brâhmanical religions. According to Fa Hian, Kapilavastu was already in the fifth century A.D. a vast wilderness of ruins; it was the same in Hiuen Tsiang's time two hundred years later. The ruins, therefore, have fortunately not been disfigured by late reconstructions, nor have the Musalmân invaders ever touched them. Systematic excavations, if conducted by the Nepâl Government on a large scale, are sure to furnish us with documents and monuments not only of the third century B. C., but of a much earlier period, extending to about the fifth and sixth centuries B. C.

Plate

GROUP OF THÂRÛ MEN.

From negatives by Bhairon Bakhsh.

GROUP OF THÂRÛ WOMEN.

Photo-etching: Survey of India Offices, Calcutta.

AŚOKA'S EDICT ON PILLAR IN THE LUMBINI GROVE. (SEE PLATE

CHAPTER VIII.

THE THÂRUS, THE MODERN DESCENDANTS OF THE ŚÂKYAS.

ALTHOUGH the Śâkyas claim to be the descendants of the mythical Âryan king Ikshvâku or Okkâka, it is not quite improbable that they were in fact primarily an aboriginal, casteless and un-Âryan tribe of Northern India. Shortly after the Buddha's demise, we find Herodot using the term Σακαι as a general designation for the various branches of the Scythian race, and the word may in all probability imply the Śâkyas or Sakkas. In any case, the Buddha's ethnical names of Śâkyamuni and Śâkyasiṁha would seem to have carried great weight, a few centuries later, with the Śakas or Indo-Scythians, in adopting the Buddhist Faith, especially under the benign rule of king Kanishka, of Śaka or Turushka race, from whom the Śaka era dates. The modern offsprings of these Śâkyas are probably the Thârus,[1] the present inhabitants of the Tarâi and the outer spurs of the Nepâlese Sub-Himâlayas, who style themselves *ban-râjas*, or "forest kings," enjoying the free and easy life of the forests. The Thârus, in fact, pretend to be the direct descendants of the Sun, and they say themselves that they were originally Râjputs, who ran away after the great fight at Hastinâpura, and who lost caste by using intoxicating liquor. Their claims to rank are, however, treated with the utmost contempt by the surrounding Hindû population, because they are an abomination to the Brâhmans, as they indulge in all the impurities of eating and drinking. And to this wandering tribe, whose customs have been only slightly modified by contact with those of the Âryan invader, are locally ascribed all the vast Buddhist brick ruins, which are found scattered all over the Tarâi. Owing to the intermarriages which have taken place within the last four or five centuries between Thâru men and the Tartar Highland women, the physiognomy of the Thâru tribe has acquired in some instances a slightly Mongolian cast, which shows itself chiefly, but not to a striking degree, in slanting eyes and high cheek-bones in some of the women and children (Plate VIII, 1 and 2); whilst in the men the physical characteristics are as a rule of the strictly Indian type. They have long, wavy hair, a dark, almost black, complexion; in stature, build and gait they are distinctly Indian and not Mongolian; nor have they any traditions which connect their origin with the Tartar Highland races. Their marriage customs are governed by the rule of tribal exogamy; in other words, the bride must not be a blood relation to the husband chosen for her, nor of the same village, but of some outside village or clan. Wife-capture is secretly practised to some extent amongst the Thârus; and this practice may explain the slightly Mongolian cast of face which has now become rather common, though not universal, among the Thâru tribe. Polygamy, divorce in the form of the expulsion from the house of the faithless wife with the approval of the council, widow marriage, and the levirate under the usual restrictions are all allowed. Divorced women can marry again like

[1] Compare also, Crooke, *The Tribes and Castes of the North-Western Provinces and Oudh*, Calcutta, 1896, Volume IV, pages 380-406.

widows, and both classes are distinguished by the title *urari*, or "selected," from women who were married as virgins by the full ritual. The social status of a married widow or *divorcée* is, however, inferior to that of a regularly-married wife; but for the purposes of succession both rank alike.

The religion of the more primitive branches of the Thârus is based on a belief in ghosts or demons *(bhûts)* lurking in the forest trees and the spirits of the dead *(prêts)*; whilst the Thârus of the plains, who have taken to agriculture, are becoming rapidly Hindûized. The women do the largest part of the sowing, weeding and harvesting; whilst the men engage in hunting and fishing, which they regard as the proper occupation of their sex. Their villages are from one to two miles distant from each other, and the houses are all made of wood or grass. The outside grass walls of each house are plastered over with red mud; they never use cowdung for this or other household purposes as is usual with the Indian people outside the jungle and forests. The houses are large, cool and commodious, and generally raised on poles, in order to protect the inmates from damp and malaria. They contain large jars of red clay in which food grains and seed rice are kept (Plate VII). Every little village is a self-governing community. Disputes are decided by a council of elders, and this is sometimes presided over by a head-man. The office of head-man or *chaudhari*, is not hereditary; the man selected is one whose age, experience and knowledge of the magical and medicinal arts entitle him to more respect than the rest; and he acquires the status of head-man by tacit consent and not by formal election. The decisions of the council or the head-man are obeyed unreservedly; litigation between Thârus and Hindûs is equally unknown. Amongst themselves the Thârus are, for the most part, a peaceful and good-natured race, following without question, as if by a law of nature, the customs and maxims of their ancestors. The honesty of the Thârus is proverbial. It is said that when a family flies into the hills, they will always leave any arrears of rent that may be due tied up in a rag to the lintel of their deserted house. Like all secluded races, the Thârus are notorious for witchcraft, and in the plains *Thâruhat* or "the Thâru country" is a synonym for witch-land. Every Thâru woman, after the marriageable age, is supposed by those who live outside the Thâru country to possess the power of the Evil Eye to bewitch and enchant: so that she has the power to turn a stranger into a wild animal or destroy him slowly by consumptive fever. This is one of the reasons why all natives of India outside the Tarâi forests dread the Thârus and fear to live amongst them.

From a negative by Bhairon Bakhsh

Photo-etching - Survey of India Offices, Calcutta, August 1897.

INTERIOR OF THÂRÛ HOUSE. (AFTER A FIRE)

CHAPTER IX.

HISTORICAL CONCLUSIONS.

For the student of Buddhism and early Indian History the discoveries already made yield some valuable results. It is now evident that the kingdom of the Śâkyas lay, as their legends recount, on the lower slopes of the Himâlayas, and that they were, as they too admit, forest and hill Râjputs exiled from the more civilized districts. Their settlement in the Tarâi and hill-forests must have separated them from their brethren further south and west. Their isolation no doubt forced them to develop the entirely non-Âryan and non-Indian custom of endogamy, as well as other habits not in accordance with those of their kindred. This explains also the reason why intermarriages between them and the other noble families of Northern India did not take place. It was not, as their tradition says, their pride of blood which prevented such alliances, but the stigma attaching to exiles who had departed from the customs of their race, and were not even free from a strong admixture of non-Âryan blood.

For the history of Aśoka, the Rummindei and Niglîvâ Pillar Edicts teach us that the Emperor in the 21st year after his coronation, or in the 25th year of his reign, visited the sacred places of the Buddhists in Northern India, at the suggestion of his spiritual adviser, Sthavira Upagupta, who alone in the whole country at that time seems to have possessed the knowledge of the whereabouts of the Lumbinî grove. Most probably Aśoka visited on this occasion not only the Lumbinî garden, Kapilavastu, the Nirvâṇa-stûpas of Buddha Koṇâgamana and Krakucchanda, but also further east the site of Gautama Buddha's *parinirvâṇa* at Kusinârâ and Râmagâma, and further west the old town of Śrâvastî, in several of which localities pillars with his inscriptions were still existing in Hiuen Tsiang's time. Aśoka's route from his capital of Pâṭaliputra towards the Tarâi is perhaps marked by the series of pillars extending from Bakhra near Vaiśalî (Besaṛh) through Radhiâ (Ararâj) and Mathiâ (Navandgaṛh) to Râmpûrvâ in the Champâran district of the Bengal Presidency, close to the Tarâi, most of which were later on inscribed with the so-called Pillar Edicts. The fact that Aśoka undertook such a journey may be interpreted as indicating that he was at that time a believing Buddhist; but it may also be looked upon as one of the *dhammayâtâs*, or "religious tours," which, according to the eighth Rock Edict, the Emperor undertook regularly since the eleventh year after his anointment, or in the fifteenth year of his reign, in order "to obtain enlightenment." The fact that he planted a number of pillars all over the Tarâi indicates that also this district belonged then to his extensive Empire.

Thus all the sacred Buddhist sites in the western portion of the Nepâlese Tarâi, mentioned by the Chinese pilgrims, have been satisfactorily identified. Some others, particularly Râmagrâma and Kusinârâ, will probably be found during the cold season of 1897-98 in the eastern portion of the Nepâlese lowlands.

I conclude this monograph with the following suitable words uttered by the wandering ascetic, Vacchagotta, in the *Majjhima-nikâya, sutta* 72:—"It is as if, oh Gautama, there were a mighty *sâl*-tree near to some village or town, and it were to lose its dead branches and twigs, and its loose shreds of bark, and its unsound wood, so that afterwards, free from those branches and twigs, and the loose shreds of bark, and the unsound wood, it were to stand neat and clean in its strength. In exactly the same way does the word of Gautama, free from branches and twigs, and from loose shreds of bark, and from unsound wood, stand neat and clean in its strength. It is as if, oh Gautama, one were to set up that which was overturned; or were to disclose that which was hidden; or were to point out the way to a lost traveller; or were to carry a lamp into a dark place, that they who have eyes might see forms. Even so has Gautama Buddha expounded the Doctrine in many ways."

THE MOGHUL ARCHITECTURE OF FATHPUR SIKRI:

By EDMUND W. SMITH,

Architectural Surveyor, N.-W. Provinces and Oudh.

Part I, with 120 Plates, Rs. 20.

Part II, with 103 Plates, Rs. 14.

Part III, with 97 Plates, Rs. 20.

ALLAHABAD:—GOVERNMENT PRESS, N.-W. P. AND OUDH.

"AT last an adequate beginning of a fairly complete and authoritative description of the magnificent buildings at and near Agra has been made. Nothing approaching to a scientific or reasonably satisfactory description of the Táj and other great edifices at Agra exists. The notices in Cunningham's Series of Archæological Reports are feeble, inane, and all but useless; and we fear that we must wait long for the costly and elaborate work which is needed to record the results of a thorough survey of the Fort, the Táj, the Mausoleum at Sikandra, and the other architectural wonders which adorn Agra and its environs. Dr. Burgess, before his retirement, decided that since it was not possible to do everything, it was more advisable to begin with Faṭhpûr-Sîkrî than with Agra itself; and it was accordingly decreed that 'the wonderful and beautiful city founded by Akbar at Faṭhpûr-Sîkrî, and often likened to Pompeii,' should be surveyed.

"In the course of four seasons Mr. Edmund W. Smith, the very capable officer in charge of the Architectural Branch of the Archæological Survey, assisted by a well trained staff of native draughtsmen, has made an elaborate survey of the Great Moghul's palace city. The first instalment of the results of his work lies before us in a handsome quarto volume, illustrated by one hundred and twenty-five full-page plates, of which some are drawings and others photo-etchings.

"The size of the work prevents its publication in one volume. The first part now published deals with the *Mahal-i-Khas*, including Akbar's bed-room, the *Panch Mahal*, the *Diwan-i-Khas*, and a few other buildings; the second part deals with Rája Bîr Bal's house and the palace of Jôdh Bai; the third will treat of Salîm Chhishti's shrine, the Turkish baths, and many other edifices; and the fourth part will be devoted to the Great Mosque. Both the third and fourth parts will be enriched with coloured illustrations of the mural decoration and inlaid work. The volume now issued contains ten coloured plates, reproducing fresco paintings and ornaments, which have been executed by Messrs. Griggs and Son with their usual skill. These frescoes attract little attention from the ordinary visitor, and are now so damaged as scarcely to repay the cost and trouble of reproduction. One of the best executed and most intelligible fragments is that on the north wall of Akbar's bed-room, which represents some passengers of distinction taking their pleasure in a sailing boat, apparently on the Jumna. The figures are well drawn in the style affected by the miniature painters. In all the drawings the perspective is very bad. Some of the paintings exhibit distinct and unmistakable traces of Chinese influence. Others seem to be imitations of Japanese motives, and several offer clear evidence of the influence exercised on Akbar's eclectic taste by Christian religious art.

"The best known of the frescoes, that on the western façade of Miriam's House, which the guide points out as a picture of the Annunciation, may possibly be intended to represent that event. But the guide's theory that Miriam, or Mary, was a Christian wife of Akbar, is unsupported by any evidence, and is opposed to the evidence that exists. The queen of Akbar who enjoyed the title of *Maryam-us-Zamani*, or 'the Mary of the age,' was really the daughter of a Hindu Rája. Akbar's mother was known by a similar title, *Maryam Makani*, and there is no more reason for believing Akbar's queen, who bore the court title of *Maryam-us-Zamani*, to have been a Christian, than there is for believing in the Christianity of his mother. In short, Akbar's Christian queen seems to be the creature of the imagination of guides greedy for *buchsheesh*. But errors fed by *bucksheesh* die hard, and Akbar's Christian queen is bound to reappear frequently for the next hundred years. The Roman Catholic priests insist on believing in her existence, and their congregations, of course, are of the same opinion.

"The celebrated throne-pillar in the *Diwan-i-Khas* is perhaps the most curious of the many marvels at Faṭhpûr. It is adequately illustrated by a dozen well-selected plates. We are by no means disposed to accept Mr. Keene's suggestion that the little building occupied by the throne-pillar is the *Ibâdat Khâna*, or hall, in which Akbar used to amuse himself with listening to set debates by the professors of rival creeds. The building is far too small for such a purpose, and does not agree well with the recorded description of the *Ibâdat Khâna*. It is more probable, as Mr. Smith observes, that the hall lay just outside the private buildings of the palace than inside their precincts, and ruins of an important building exist near the Record Office in a position which would have been very suitable for a hall such as is described by the contemporary historian.

"We must not linger longer over the beauties of Akbar's magnificent, though singularly uncomfortable, palace. We can recommend Mr. Smith's book as an excellent piece of work, thoroughly well done; and can assure our readers that merely as a picture book it is good value for twenty rupees. The printing and paper are first-rate. The binding, alas! is of the worst possible quality, and not even fit for a report by a Board of Revenue. When the next part comes out the Local Government should follow the example of Bombay and treat its pretty pictures to safe and decent covering."—*The Pioneer*, 12*th July* 1895.

"THE first volume is now before us, and it may be truly said that nothing more interesting or artistic has been published for a long time by the Indian Government . . . The hundred and twenty large quarto plans, views, and details are excellently reproduced . . . No architect or artist, and certainly no student of Mediæval India, can sufficiently prize the results . . ."—*Morning Post*, 4*th November* 1895.

"THIS volume is welcomed as the first instalment of a more complete illustration of a single important group of Indian sixteenth-century buildings than it has hitherto been able to publish . . . It is most desirable we should have as complete architectural drawings of the more famous buildings in India as we have of those in France, Italy, and other Western countries; and amongst these the Muhammadan architecture, in Upper India especially, presents some splendid examples. Every traveller is familiar with those at Agra, Delhi, and Fathpûr-Sîkrî; and many visit a place so unique as the latter in its history, in Indian architecture, and present condition . . . The value of this work lies in these numerous and careful drawings, which afford a full representation of the buildings surveyed and of the marvellous richness of their details . . . With this work before him, the student of architecture and Oriental art may judge what a wealth of further information would be afforded were a few other groups of buildings, such as those around Agra and Delhi, &c., similarly surveyed and delineated, while like surveys were made at Abu, Tanjor, Worangal, and elsewhere in the Peninsula . . ."—*Journal of the Royal Institute of British Architects*, 21*st November* 1895.

"MR. E. W. SMITH has published the second part of his monumental work on Fathpûr-Sîkrî. We noticed the first part at some length in these columns last year, and need only say that the second part is equally beautiful and well executed."—*Pioneer*, 10*th December* 1896.

"EVERY traveller in India knows the deserted city of Fathpûr-Sîkrî, within the seven-mile circuit of which is gathered that strangely beautiful medley of buildings, of all styles and plans, and destined for every sort of purpose, which has long been the delight and marvel of artists and architects. That stern critic, James Fergusson, when he stood amongst the empty courts and palaces of the silent city, could only bow down and worship in the terminology of his craft. How keenly he would have enjoyed that admirable volume of drawings and descriptions which Mr. E. W. Smith has consecrated to the remains of Akbar's escurial in the 'Imperial Series' of Reports of the Archæological Survey of India. Mr. Smith need not, we think, be under any apprehension that a single qualified critic will find fault with his work on the ground that 'unnecessary labour has been bestowed' upon it.

"It is impossible to speak in too high praise of the accuracy and beauty of the 120 plates contained in the present instalment. Mr. Smith has displayed sound judgment in his selection of subjects.

"The work has been ably seconded by Colonel Waterhouse and his Assistants of the Survey of India Office, where the plans and drawings have been ably reproduced. The photo-etchings are really exquisite.

"Mr. Grigg, too, has shown his usual ability in reproducing the effects of the coloured decorations."—*The Athæneum*, 26*th October* 1895.

EPIGRAPHIA INDICA

and Record of the Archæological Survey of India.

Edited by JAS. BURGESS, C.I.E., LL.D., F.R.S.E.;

Assisted by A. FÜHRER, PH. D., *Archæological Surveyor, N.-W. Provinces and Oudh.*

Volume I (1891). Super-royal 4to, 482 pages, with 35 facsimile Plates. Rs. 16.

Volume II (1894). Super-royal 4to, 518 pages, with 51 facsimile Plates. Rs. 16.

Edited by DR. E. HULTZSCH, Government Epigraphist.

Volume III (1894-95), 4to, 393 pages, with 38 facsimile Plates. Rs. 24.

Published under the authority of the Government of India as a Supplement to the *Indian Antiquary.*

CALCUTTA:—SUPERINTENDENT OF GOVERNMENT PRINTING, INDIA.

"L'idée de réunir en une publication spéciale les inscriptions de plus en plus nombreuses et à mesure qu'elles sont mises au jour par les diverses branches de l'Archæological Survey, est excellente. Il était temps que l'Inde eût à son tour son *Ephemeris Palæographica.*"—A. BARTH.